JONATHAN ADLER

MY PRESCRIPTION FOR

ANTI-DEPRESSIVE LIVING

JONATHAN ADLER

MY PRESCRIPTION FOR
ANTI-DEPRESSIVE LIVING

WITH ORIGINAL PHOTOGRAPHS BY ANNIE SCHLECHTER

PUBLISHED BY

ReganBooks
An Imprint of HarperCollinsPublishers

PRODUCED BY

MELCHER
MEDIA

THIS BOOK WAS PRODUCED BY

 **MELCHER MEDIA**

124 WEST 13TH STREET
NEW YORK, NY 10011
WWW.MELCHER.COM

PUBLISHER: CHARLES MELCHER
ASSOCIATE PUBLISHER: BONNIE ELDON
EDITOR IN CHIEF: DUNCAN BOCK
PRODUCTION DIRECTOR: ANDREA HIRSH
PROJECT EDITOR: MEGAN WORMAN
EDITORIAL ASSISTANT: LAUREN NATHAN

DESIGNED BY YAEL EISELE

PHOTO CREDITS, CONSTITUTING AN EXTENSION
OF THE COPYRIGHT PAGE, APPEAR ON PAGE 198.

FOR INFORMATION ADDRESS
HARPERCOLLINS PUBLISHERS INC.
10 EAST 53RD STREET
NEW YORK, NY 10022

PRINTED IN CHINA
ISBN-10 0-06-082053-5
ISBN-13 978-0-06-082053-4

. . .

for simon

CONTENTS

...

FOREWORD

Regarding my partnership with Jonathan Adler, I am afraid I can make no startling revelations or lurid disclosures. Sorry about that. Our ten-year relationship is completely free of tawdry shenanigans and horrid addictions. We have never tried to poison one another's food or vindictively unravel a favorite sweater. Simply put, we are a HAPPY COUPLE.

I am well aware that this might sound a bit suburban and smug, but it happens to be the truth. We are a happy couple. Jonathan and I contentedly spend most of our waking and nonwaking hours together. We are each other's FAVORITE PERSON and preferred dinner date. We become peevish if we cannot sit together at functions, and we never travel anywhere without each other if we can help it.

In a world where it has become WILDLY UNCHIC to speak in mushy and enthusiastic terms about one's significant other, and where most couples seem intent on divorcing and/or murdering each other, Jonathan and I are something of an anomaly.

To what do I attribute the strange success of our happy union?

We don't really have very much in common: he's a Jew, I'm not; he eats meat, I prefer seaweed; I'm middle-aged, he's not; I like highbrow, pretentious European movies, and he would rather watch *The Terminator*.

So what is the source of the cosmic fairy-dust which keeps us in each other's thrall?

It might sound insane, but I am convinced that the key to our happiness might well be found in our DÉCOR! Yes, our interior decoration!

As can be imagined, our home is filled with everything Jonathan Adler. Every room is crammed with textiles and ceramics in bold Adlerian colors and intriguing shapes. We live surrounded by Jonathan's design and craft. The happy chic of his diverse oeuvre fills every nook and cranny of our pad.

No matter how grim my day, when I come home and plop my keys into the Adler vase that sits on the chartreuse lacquer hall table, toss my hat on the $5 Michael Jackson bust that Jonathan found at the 26th Street flea market, and collapse onto the graphic alpaca rug to play with the dog, the CARES AND FRUSTRATIONS of the day melt away as if I had just downed a large scotch. Ditto Jonathan.

As we putz around our home, the upbeat nuances of his aesthetic work their magic on our souls; a feeling of squishy contentment enrobes us and vanquishes the impulse to bicker and taunt. (Apologies again for being uncool and mushy.)

I know what you're thinking: "Simon Doonan has obviously had some kind of break with reality. He actually believes that interior design—Adler design in particular—is the key to a successful relationship!"

CALL ME A LUNATIC if you will, but I'm standing my ground, and more than willing to allow any naysayer to test my hypothesis. Go ahead!

Why not try the following experiment: Simply transplant Jonathan and myself into an alternative environment and observe our behavioral changes with surveillance cameras, à la *Big Brother*. How would our relationship fare if we were placed, for example, in a RIGOROUSLY MINIMAL abode with beige marble floors, beige ultrasuede banquettes, and pompous, highly provenanced furniture?

There is no doubt in my mind as to how this scenario would play out. After one day in this beautiful-but-dour environment, we would begin to disintegrate into a state of Pinter-esque angst. After a week or so of this décor-deprivation, we would be so starved of GORGEOUS COLOR and GROOVY DESIGN that we would begin clawing at the venetian plaster walls and gnawing on the furniture, and then each other, but not in an affectionate way.

So, let that be a warning to you, all you young hopefuls who think you may have met the person of your dreams! SURROUND YOURSELF WITH ADLER HAPPY CHIC, OR SINK INTO A MATRIMONIAL SWAMP!

Best wishes,

Simon Doonan

THIS BOOK IS ABOUT HOW INTERIOR DECORATING CAN CHANGE YOUR LIFE

Yes, you heard me, change your life. *My Prescription for Anti-Depressive Living* is a therapeutic intervention designed to rescue you from whatever decorating diseases you are struggling with. Inside this book you will find homes I have decorated and products I have designed. You will also find strong opinions, wayward rants, and lots of very cute pictures of my Norwich Terrier, Liberace.

My hope is to give you, *cher readeur*, a transfusion of joy, abandon, and creativity in decorating your home. Adulthood can make you too serious. Modern technology can burn you out. Daily routines can make you give up on your dreams of grandeur. There are remedies for these ailments, and the remedies are at your fingertips, with the help of *Moi*, some courage, and pluck. Your home can be the antidote to the heartaches and traumas of everyday life.

I want you to walk in your front door every day and feel happy.

MINIMALISM
IS A BUMMER:

Be Immoderate and Be Happy

...

HAPPINESS
IS CHIC

A few years ago, Simon, Liberace, and I needed a little getaway, so we ensconced our-selves in a fancy-pants Caribbean resort. We had been reading about it ad nauseam in the haute-couture magazines that we're all supposed to read. The design community had heralded it as a breathtaking example of minimalist perfection—spare, Germanic, intellectual. Lemming-like, we rushed to sample its splendid style sensibility. The guests matched the décor: They were appropriate, restrained, and quite hushed. Although it was unimpeachably tasteful, something was missing.

On the first afternoon, clad in our resort ensembles, we took an appropriate stroll down the beach and stumbled upon the adjacent resort: a massive, seemingly endless extrava-ganza of casinos, water slides, and themed restaurants. Our hotel was gray; this hotel was pink. Everywhere we looked, revelers were flying past on jet skis, swimming through shark tanks, and guzzling brightly colored umbrella drinks. Nothing could have been more antithetical to the resort where we were staying. Our resort was intimidatingly mini-mal, while this hotel was infectiously maximal—exuberant, ornate, fun. It was all that my window-dressing husband could do not to run back to our hotel room and staple up some tinsel. In a stunning epiphany, we realized the utter pointlessness of good taste without fun. Here were two polar opposite sensibilities that somehow needed to be fused. There, on the spot, I decided that I needed to make this my lifelong mission: to meld happiness with chicness—and then inflict my vision on the world.

NOTHING SAYS *BONJOUR* LIKE A GIANT CERAMIC DOG. THIS FRIENDLY *CHIEN* SITS RIGHT NEXT TO THE DOOR IN MY PALM BEACH PAD, AND MY MOOD IS ALWAYS BRIGHTENED THE MINUTE I STEP INSIDE.

your home should be like a good dose of Zoloft

A chic home isn't one that's filled with uncomfortable furniture and art that you don't understand. It's a home filled with things that you love and that make you happy. Coming home should be an antidote to the troubles and traumas of everyday life. It should be like hearing your favorite song on the car radio, a first kiss, running into your ex-boyfriend and he's fat, being the 100th caller. It shouldn't feel like Sunday night, doing your taxes, eating fiber, or getting your teeth cleaned. I'm here to tell you that good home decorating can be the equivalent of years of therapy.

live lavishly in a squishy bedroom

Hotel-ish comfort is hip. Check yourself into a world of opulent fabrics, gorgeous surfaces, and expensive presents. Take your bedding to the limit. Luxuriate in matching linens, drapes, headboards, and pantsuits. Pamper your paws with fluffy carpet. (What's so great about wood floors, anyway?) People who deny themselves comfort and luxury baffle me. Why punish yourself? Your bedroom should feel like the most luxurious hotel room in the world.

OPPOSITE PAGE: THIS IS THE LOBBY OF THE
PARKER, A HOTEL IN PALM SPRINGS THAT I
GAVE A HEAD-TO-TOE MAKEOVER. THE ETHNIC
TAPESTRIES ON THE SOFAS ARE CALLED *SUZANIS*,
AND THEY WERE MADE IN UZBEKISTAN. I LOVE
THE FACT THAT THEY'RE SO LOUD AND COLORFUL
BUT ALSO CASUAL AND INVITING. THE ARTWORK
IS BY ONE OF MY FAVORITE PAINTERS, JOHN
KACERE, WHO'S KNOWN FOR HIS PHOTOREALIST
PAINTINGS OF WOMEN IN PANTIES. THE CHAN-
DELIER IS BY ARTELUCE, THE SUBLIME ITALIAN
LIGHTING CONCERN, AND THE CHAIRS ARE BY
GIO PONTI.

be inappropriate

Modesty is overrated. Let the world know just how naughty you are—what do you have
to lose? And you don't need to spend years in Freudian analysis to get in
touch with your id. Just hang a painting of purple panties in your living room or put
a vase covered in squillions of breasts in your foyer to let guests know who
they're dealing with. We all have a wild side, but we're taught to hide it. Use decorating
to unleash your sizzle on the world.

THIS HOUSE, DESIGNED BY MODERNIST ICON BERTRAND GOLDBERG, IS MADE OF BEAUTIFUL MATERIALS LIKE FIELDSTONE WALLS AND MAHOGANY CEILINGS. I PUNCTUATED THE STRONG, ORGANIC ELEMENTS WITH BURSTS OF COLOR AND FUN—A BRASS RHINOCEROS, A RED VLADIMIR KAGAN SOFA, AND A TRIPPY POP-ART PAINTING.

go for grandeur with a giant chandelier and a brass rhinoceros

I believe in bold gestures. Got a small apartment? Name it Worthington Arms and emblazon the name on everything: matchbooks, stationery, Tupperware. Rococo house? Buy mod furniture. No money? Road trip. I think that people err on the side of tastefulness rather than boldness, often with negative consequences. I don't want to look back on my life and think about the things I should have done. Of course, you might say that home décor isn't going to make or break you psychologically, and you'd be right. I encourage you to be bold in every arena of your life.

mix and match with panache

Don't be tentative with patterns. You only go around once, and you want to look back on your life and remember the brocade walls, not the white lampshades. If you keep your color scheme restrained, you can approach patterns with wild abandon. When in doubt, repeat, repeat, repeat.

find inspiration

For my Muse collection, I used body parts rather than geometric shapes to create patterns in relief. Although geometric patterns were my signature style, one day I was sitting at the kitchen table with my window-dresser husband and noticed that he had a mannequin head in front of him (as he often does). The head was right next to one of my pots, but my eye was drawn to the mannequin. I realized that there is something innately compelling about faces, perhaps because we all want to make human contact. It was a "Eureka!" moment. I immediately ran to my studio and threw some pots applied with rows of lips, breasts, and eyes. With their unglazed porcelain finish, my Muse pots have an ethereal and surreal character. Each pot is named for a muse who inspired one of the great surrealist artists.

OPPOSITE PAGE: SIMON, LIBERACE, AND I LOVE TO CHILL OUT AT OUR SHELTER ISLAND BEACH HOUSE.

be true to yourself

In spite of my bossy tone and deep-seated belief that I am always right, I think it's important to follow your own vision about what makes you happy and to live your own life. I learned this lesson the hard way. (See "The Story of Moi" for the full details of my rocky journey.) When I was in college and madly in love with pottery and desperately hoping to make a career of it, my pottery professor told me that I had no talent as a potter and that I should consider law school. I am so happy every day that I didn't listen. The minute I stopped listening to other people was the minute that I became the most creative and prolific and full of joy. You know in your heart what you love and what makes you happy, so listen to yourself. Or listen to me— I'm happy either way.

"HELLO, I'D LIKE TO ORDER SOME MORE CLAY."

My Prescription For :
MAXIMALIST MERRIMENT

1. OVERTIP!

3. PLAY WITH PAINT. BUY A JERE WALL SCULPTURE AND PAINT A **RECTANGLE OF COLOR** BEHIND IT AS A FRAME.

2. PUT A CANOPY OVER YOUR BED FOR MAJESTIC SLUMBER. YOU CAN DO IT AD HOC, WITH A FLOWY, HIPPIE MOSQUITO NET, OR **BE REGAL** WITH AN ORNATE LOUIS XIV CORONET. DON'T SETTLE FOR A QUOTIDIAN BED.

4. DECORATE OUTSIDE OF THE BOX. **DANGLE A HANGING CHAIR** IN YOUR LIVING ROOM, PUT BEADED CURTAINS IN DOORWAYS, PLOP A SUIT OF ARMOR IN YOUR FOYER. AMUSE YOURSELF.

5. GET RID OF ALL OF YOUR BORING, TIRESOME FRIENDS. **MAKE FRIENDS WITH CABARET STARS,** EXOTIC DANCERS, AND DOWN-ON-THEIR-LUCK ROYALTY INSTEAD.

6. DON'T FIT IN. SCALE IS THE MOST UNDER-CONSIDERED PIECE OF THE **DECORATING PUZZLE.** PUT A MILKING STOOL IN A MASSIVE PALAZZO OR A GOTHIC THRONE IN A STUDIO APARTMENT.

8. LAYER, LAYER, LAYER. UNEXPECTED TOUCHES ARE THE SOUL OF THE **MAXIMALIST HOME**— A PAINTING HUNG ON A BOOKCASE, A CHAN-DELIER IN A CLOSET, A BRASS LION'S-HEAD DOOR KNOCKER IN A MODERN APARTMENT.

7. COMPLIMENT LAVISHLY. TELL SOMEONE WHO THEIR CELEBRITY LOOK-ALIKE IS. GREET EFFUSIVELY. **BE FRIENDLIER** THAN YOU THINK YOU SHOULD BE.

...

GO STARK RAVING MOD:

Groovy Graphics and Pop Paraphernalia

"WHAT WOULD MRS. GOLDSTEIN DO?"

The Goldsteins were my next-door neighbors and best friends growing up in suburban New Jersey, and their house was the ne plus ultra of fabulous modern decorating. I have always been completely obsessed with Mrs. Goldstein's style. Often, when I am making something groovy, I think to myself "How would this look chez Goldstein?" Allow me to describe chez Goldstein.

In the foyer was a giant Murano light fixture hanging over a pop-art painting of a gorilla. The kitchen walls were découpaged (by Mrs. G. herself) in *New Yorker* magazine covers. The den had a George Nelson sectional sofa upholstered in bright red, which was surrounded with African art, groovy C. Jere wall sculptures, and a Knoll coffee table supporting a giant sculpture of a hippopotamus. The living room was heaven. In one corner was a black lacquered piano with a ceramic leopard under it sitting on a white flokati rug. The coffee table was mirrored, the sofa-back table was covered in snakeskin, and on a shelf there was a ceramic piece of cake.

It was all put together with a sense of panache and confidence that I strive to equal to this day. Nothing was chosen to blend in—everything took center stage. Basically, the lesson I learned from Mrs. Goldstein was to be graphic, bold, and confident, and to put things in your home that make you happy. As born-again Christians ask themselves when confronted with a dilemma, "What would Jesus do?" so I ask myself, "What would Mrs. Goldstein do?"

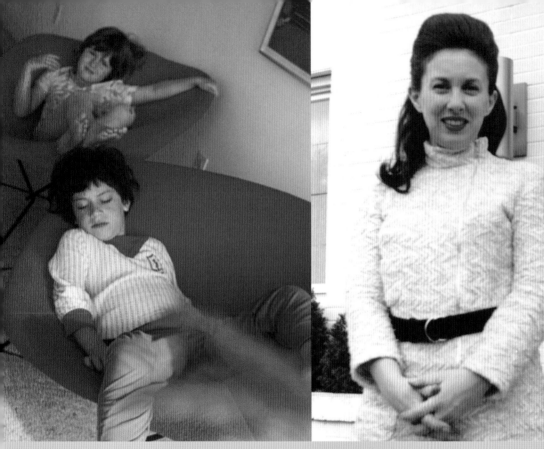

ABOVE LEFT: HERE ARE ANDREW GOLDSTEIN AND *MOI* CAVORTING ON A PAIR OF BERTOIA DIAMOND CHAIRS, WHICH ARE REPRISED IN MY PALM BEACH HOME, OPPOSITE. **ABOVE RIGHT:** THIS IS NOT THE ÜBER-CHIC FASHION DESIGNER MIUCCIA PRADA, IT'S MRS. GOLDSTEIN CIRCA 1968 (ACTUALLY, MRS. G. IS MUCH MORE CHIC). **OPPOSITE PAGE:** THIS ROOM REFLECTS A WEIRD CONVERGENCE OF A LOT OF MY FAVORITE OBJECTS: A NEEDLEPOINT PILLOW OF A VINTAGE MODEL T, A BJORN WIINBLAD CANDLE HOLDER, AND A BERTOIA CHAIR ON A ZEBRA RUG—ALL PRESIDED OVER BY THE HAUNTING VISAGE IN A PAINTING BY LATIN AMERI-CAN ARTIST JUAN CALOGERO.

exude exuberance

If you've got a bad case of Seriousitis, pop style can be just the electric shock therapy you need. The symptoms of Seriousitis include boredom, fatigue, excessive appropri-ateness, and complete loss of *joie de vivre*. Pop is about clean lines, bold colors, and a sense of humor. It's the antidote to taking yourself and your life too seriously. Paint a wall orange, needlepoint ornery messages onto pillows, cancel your subscription to the *Wall Street Journal* and pick up *MAD* magazine instead.

IN THE UPSTAIRS SLEEPING LOFT OF OUR
SHELTER ISLAND PAD, WE DECIDED TO HAVE A
PINK-AND-PURPLE, PSYCHEDELIC VICTORIANA FREAK-
OUT. IN THE SITTING AREA, I COMBINED A WROUGHT-
IRON VICTORIAN LAMP, A RUG WITH AN ORNATE
SCROLLY MOTIF, AND MOD PIERRE PAULIN CHAIRS IN
MIND-ALTERING PURPLE THAT I FOUND AT A PARIS
FLEA MARKET. IN THE GUEST ROOM, I DESIGNED A
CUSTOM-WOVEN SPREAD. AND IN THE WORK AREA,
I PAINTED THE FLOOR MAGENTA, PERCHED A GIANT
SNAIL ON A CHAIR, AND HUNG A COLLECTION OF OVER-
SIZE KEYS ON THE WALL.

psychedelic victoriana

When you think of Victoriana, you probably think of doilies. But when I think of Victoriana, my pulse quickens and I think of that time in the '60s when psychedelia met Art Nouveau and everyone had fun.

For me, Victoriana used to evoke tragic B&Bs: piles of lacy pillows on daybeds and seasonally dressed stuffed bears looking sadly down on guest sign-in books. I was always confounded by the people who gave up their corporate lives to create perpetually "homey" environments for an endless parade of strangers. I imagined them decanting cereals into fusty glass jars, wondering why they felt more alienated than ever. Twee B&Bs too closely resemble Victorian times, and what was so great about Victorian times, anyway? Skirts covered piano legs because they were too sexual; soot belched from smokestacks; corsets mangled pancreases; *Will & Grace* hadn't been born yet. Victoriana equaled frumpiana.

But then came purple! When some geniuses in the '60s decided to take down the establishment, they turned the symbols of propriety on their heads. What could be more subversive than painting the iconography of Victorian England purple? In London, people used claw-footed bathtubs as chaises. Oversize pince-nez eyeglasses became wall art. In San Francisco, Victorian houses glistened with pink paint, while on the walls inside, rock posters married Art Nouveau style with LSD. Chicks wore high-necked crotch-length governess frocks while practicing free love. Everyone had a blast.

So now when I think of Victoriana, it puts a smile on my face. The political agenda of the '60s has faded somewhat, but the idea of turning frumpy into fun is one of the great legacies of the counterculture.

29

THE BAR IN THE PARKER LOBBY IS DELUXE. THE FLOOR IS GREEN MARBLE, AND THE WALLS HAVE BRONZE MIRROR INSETS. MY CHALLENGE WAS TO KEEP THE FANCY FEELING BUT MAKE IT FROLIC-SOME AT THE SAME TIME. SO, I CHOSE FIXTURES AND ACCESSORIES THAT ARE AS DRESSY AS THE SHELL OF THE BAR (THE SCONCES ARE '60S ITALIAN, THE PORCELAIN HORSE-AND-CARRIAGE IS 19TH-CENTURY BAVARIAN) BUT THAT ARE IMPROBABLE AND SURREAL AND PLAYFUL.

go from fancy to frisky

A mod sensibility isn't only about futur-
istic fashion and space-age silhouettes.
Mod is a state of mind. It's about bring-
ing a frisky frisson to serious spaces.
It's about unexpected gestures. Mod is
about fun.

THERE WAS AN AWKWARD SHELF ON A DRAB, WHITE WALL IN THE PARKER. SO I TROLLED EVERY THRIFT STORE IN THE DESERT LOOKING FOR BRIGHTLY COLORED GLASS AND CREATED THIS POP-Y, HAPPY FRIEZE.

when you have your picture taken, rent a white poodle and eat Froot Loops—they're more photogenic than oatmeal.

THIS PAGE: IN MY BEDDING COLLECTION, I LOVE
TO MIX DIFFERENT PATTERNS IN MATCHING COLORS.
OPPOSITE PAGE: HERE, THE DARK COLOR
SCHEME OF THE BROWN GRASS-CLOTH WALL IS
LEAVENED BY A JOLT OF PINK AND ORANGE. THE
GIANT PINK PAINTING IS BY AN ARTIST CALLED
CANDY ASS, WHO DEFINITELY HAS SOME CONCEPT
THAT HE'S WORKING, ALTHOUGH I DON'T UNDER-
STAND IT. I JUST LOVE THAT IT'S A BIG FIELD OF PINK.

banish the blues with pink and orange

At the Adler Laboratories on Hudson Street, NYC, we've made a very important scientific discovery: Pink and orange, combined liberally, raise the serotonin levels in your brain, creating euphoria.

replace Prozac with
perky pop patterns

live life inside out

The pool pavilion at The Parker, above, feels like a groovy outdoor living room. It's the perfect place to lounge around in a caftan and pretend to be an early '70s glamourpuss like Bianca Jagger or Talitha Getty.

The canopy over the restaurant terrace, opposite, epitomizes the cheeky cheerfulness of California. The vivid palette is inspired by the bougainvillea that surround the property. The oranges and yellows of the fabric reflect the many moods of the sun, while the colored cushions add a layer of fun to the classic Bertoia chairs.

trap the sunshine with yellow and chrome

We painted our Palm Beach bedroom bright yellow because it's the color of the sun, so we always wake up in a good mood. The four-poster bed is a bit of sparkling brilliance by the mid-century designer Paul Evans. We bought it at an antique store in New York (it is the major splurge in the room), and we found the giant carved silver dollar at a thrift store in Palm Beach. A friend told us that it was not good feng shui to hang a dollar above the bed, as you are supposed to hang something inspirational. Had I known that, I would have hung a hundred-dollar bill instead.

WORSHIP YOUR MUSES:

Andy Warhol

When I was growing up, I always dreaded going to art museums. Why look at dreary portraits of long-dead strangers when the magic of TV was at my fingertips? Wouldn't you rather tuck into a good episode of *Rhoda* than look at a painting by Willem de Kooning? Then, one day, my parents dragged me kicking and screaming to the Philadelphia Museum of Art to see an Andy Warhol exhibition. The moment I laid my eyes on Warhol's oeuvre, my life changed. I realized that art could be better than TV.

Warhol's art was fun and playful and serious and gorgeous and shocking and high and low and postmodern when modern was cool. He was the first artist to understand our celebrity-obsessed popular culture and both mock it and celebrate it at the same time. When I look at the art world today, I get pretty depressed. I think that some-where along the way, people were tricked into believing that art has to be incomprehensible and skill-free and ugly. I totally reject that idea. I want my work to be communicative and beautiful and, I hope, impactful on an emotional level before an intellectual level.

In my rare moments of despair, the moments when I think that I need to be dour and obscurantist in order to be taken seriously, I just think of Andy Warhol and smile.

• • •

MY STUDIO 54 NEEDLEPOINT PILLOWS
ARE AN HOMAGE TO A BYGONE HEDONISTIC SCENE
RENDERED IN A PARADOXICALLY COZY MEDIUM.

Playlist

RENT: *SMASHING TIME*
PRACTICE: LOOKING SINCERE IN YOUR BATHROOM MIRROR
LISTEN: TO THE ROLLING STONES' *SOME GIRLS*
SHAG: YOUR BEST MATE'S GIRL

make mischief

The loveable cad who lives in this room stayed out late last night, got arrested, lost his keys, and had to climb in over the balcony. But he's always forgiven for his naughty ways. His countless girlfriends can't resist his heartfelt apologies and armfuls of flowers—he just can't help himself!

Actually, I designed this room for the Hamptons Showcase, and the loveable cad is only a figment of my imagination, an inspiration for creating an energy-infused, youth-enhancing, mischief-instigating setting for action and fun. Warning: If this room makes you feel young and carefree, I can't be held responsible for the consequences.

47

MAKE THE MOST OF MINIMALISM.
THIS HOUSE IN THE HOLLYWOOD HILLS IS SLEEK
AND MODERN, WITH CEMENT FLOORS AND WHITE
WALLS. THE FURNITURE PLAN IS SIMPLE AND
RESTRAINED LIKE THE ARCHITECTURE, BUT A FEW
PLAYFUL TOUCHES—A TWINKLY LUCITE COFFEE
TABLE, GIANT CERAMIC GREYHOUNDS, A DASH OF
BLACK—INJECT A DOSE OF HOLLYWOOD GLAMOUR.

My Prescription For :
POP PLEASURE

1. DRESS LIKE A BACK-UP SINGER.

2. ORANGE! THE POPPIEST COLOR IS THE ANSWER TO MOST DECORATING CONUNDRUMS. PAINT YOUR HAT STAND **ORANGE**, BUY AN **ORANGE** PLASTIC ARTEMIDE TABLE LAMP (WWW. ARTEMIDE.US), SERVE YOUR GUESTS FANTA. **ORANGE** MAKES AN OLD PAD ZIPPY. FYI, "SAFETY ORANGE" SPRAY PAINT FROM KRYLON IS THE PERFECT COLOR.

3. PAINT YOUR FLOORS WHITE. YOU'LL FEEL EMMA PEEL-ISH. YOU'LL FEEL **CAREFREE**. YOU'LL FEEL THINNER THAN YOU ACTUALLY ARE.

4. WOW YOUR POSSE BY LEARNING SOME OBSCURE **'60S DANCES:** THE FRUG, THE LOCOMOTION, THE HITCHHIKER, RENT SWEET CHARITY AND MEMORIZE THE MOVES FROM THE NIGHTCLUB SCENE.

6. THINK BIG! PERCH A FIVE-FOOT-TALL TOOTHBRUSH IN YOUR BATHROOM CORNER (WWW.THINKBIGNY.COM) OR A **GIANT LIGHT BULB** CHANDELIER OVER YOUR DINING-ROOM TABLE. POP STYLE IS ABOUT TOYING WITH REALITY AND HAVING FUN.

5. **SUPERGRAPHICS!** THIS '70S PHENOM- ENON LOOKS REALLY FRESH TODAY. PAINT BOLD YELLOW, BROWN, AND RED STRIPES ON THE WALL THAT CON- TINUE UNABATED OVER THE FURNITURE AND ONTO THE FLOOR.

7. VERNER PANTON. THIS MOD MASTER'S DESIGNS ARE STILL AVAILABLE AND STILL GREAT. PANTON'S WORK WAS **COLORFUL AND GRAPHIC** AND COUNTERCULTURAL. A DASH OF PANTON DOES MORE FOR YOUR HEART RATE THAN A 10K RUN. AN EBAY SEARCH OF PANTON WILL LEAD YOU TO A CORNUCOPIA OF COOL COLLECTIBLES.

8. WHEN YOU **THROW A PARTY** (AND YOU *SHOULD* THROW A PARTY, BY THE WAY), PUT *A CLOCKWORK ORANGE* ON THE TV ON A CONSTANT LOOP.

...

COLORS CAN'T CLASH:

Impudent Shades and Happy Hues

THE
PHANTOM
CLUB

When I was in the sixth grade, my older brother Dave and my older sister Amy set up a clubhouse in our basement. It was called the Phantom Club, and its sole mission was to exclude me from it. Only executives of the club were allowed to see the inside. Amy and Dave were the executives, while I was the executive assistant. As such, my responsibilities included getting lemonade for the executives, making social arrangements with the next-door neighbors, and carefully guarding the door from predators. I did it all faithfully and loyally, naïvely hoping to someday become an executive through hard work and commitment.

I never actually saw the inside of the Phantom Club. I was told that it was all purples and oranges and pinks—very lounge-y and *I Dream of Jeannie*–ish. Apparently, there were bean bag chairs, and candles cast a flattering glow. To this day, I still can't stop thinking about the mythical majesty of the Phantom Club interior. My passion for decorating other people's homes may come from a longing to re-create the lost glamour of the Phantom Club and to finally find myself on the inside.

The over-the-top spirit of the Phantom Club, in my mind's eye, is where I got all of my ideas about color. I used to try to imagine just how bold and gorgeous it was. The idea of mixing together all those wild and rich colors seemed like the apotheosis of fun.

Years later, my brother and sister told me that the Phantom Club was actually nothing special, just a few old sofa cushions, a flashlight, and photographs of the founding members on the walls. Sometimes I think it's better to hold on to your fantasies.

crank up your mood with cheery chartreuse

When I say colors can't clash, I only half mean it. What I really mean is that I love color in abundance and I abhor the dearth of it that's so prevalent in today's decorating.

Color is the cure for many psychological woes. It's nearly impossible to be gloomy in a persimmon bathroom or to be stressed out in a sage breakfast room. Color is the most accessible, over-the-counter, mood-altering substance I can think of. Overdose on color.

red, white, and blue are good for you

The year was 1976, and the Freedom Train was chugging across America. The Bicentennial lit up our country with pride and patriotism. All of America was painted red, white, and blue. For me, these are the colors of optimism. They create an instant feeling that everything is going to be okay. Unfortunately, this triumphant color scheme has been relegated to boys' rooms, although I think it should be used everywhere. What could be more KAPOW than a red, white, and blue foyer or den? Why not tuck in at night in a red, white, and blue master bedroom and wake up invigorated?

chill out with moss and rust

You don't have to get too hung up on matching colors perfectly. In this living room, I used complementary colors—green and orange—as well as my two faves—white and chocolate brown—to create a sense of harmony. The shades of orange and green are all slightly different, but it doesn't really matter. The ceramic foo dogs are from a thrift store. Decorating tip: Whenever you see two foo dogs, just buy them.

paint every-thing white and then add color with abandon

Our Shelter Island house represents pure fun to me and is the embodiment of my belief that colors can't clash. The house was originally built in 1972 by a Pan Am pilot, and when we bought it, it was in a terrible state of disrepair. The previous owner had given it a country-cottage make-over and a Santa Fe terra-cotta hearth. But we could tell that the house wanted to shed its country dreariness and come back to life. So, in the main rooms, we painted everything white: floors, ceilings, walls, and aforementioned country hearth. Then we added color everywhere.

63

take it down a notch
with honeyed hues and
golden tones

green and brown make the world go 'round

Think about it: Green and brown are the colors of nature, and nature is divine—rich, earthy, and fecund. I'm obsessed with the color brown, whether it occurs in nature or not. Brown goes with everything. Brown and baby blue? Incredibly chic. Brown and pink? Gorgeous. Brown and orange? Hermès, Hermès, Hermès. Come to think of it, maybe it's just brown that makes the world go 'round. Join the Brown Brigade!

OPPOSITE PAGE: THE BATHROOMS AT THE PARKER WERE DREARY, BUT THIS BLACK-AND-TAUPE GEO-METRIC WALLPAPER BROUGHT THEM TO LIFE. NOTHING IS FIERCER THAN BOLD WALLPAPER IN A TINY POWDER ROOM. THE PICTURE OVER THE TOILET IS A RON GALELLA IMAGE OF TRUMAN CAPOTE AT HIS INFAMOUS BLACK AND WHITE BALL. *J'ADORE* PICTURES OVER TOILETS.

whomp it up with wallpaper

Don't forget wallpaper. Sometimes paint just isn't enough for a room, and patterns can add a little pizzazz. Vintage wall-papers abound on eBay, so you have no excuse not to seek them out. And don't ignore your ceilings—wallpaper overhead adds an unexpected layer and changes a boring old ceiling from an eyesore into an eye-catcher.

THIS PAGE: THIS LITTE BOY'S BATHROOM HAS A JAUNTY NAUTICAL THEME. THE ROOM LACKED A WINDOW, SO THE PORTHOLE LEADING TO THE HALLWAY ADDS LIGHT AND OPENNESS. **OPPOSITE PAGE:** IN THE ADJOINING BEDROOM, GOLD AND BLUE RULE. THE TRIUMPHANT AWNING AND STRIPED WALLS CREATE A FORT FIT FOR A PETIT PRINCE.

THIS LITTLE GIRL'S ROOM IS FUN AND OVER THE TOP: CRAZY VINTAGE WALLPAPER, A PINK GINGHAM CANOPY, AND A QUEEN ANNE HIGHBOY DRESSER LACQUERED LIME GREEN, ALL ANCHORED BY CHOCOLATE BROWN CARPETING. KIDS' ROOMS ARE SO DERANGED AND VISUALLY STIMULATING—I WISH ADULTS WOULD HAVE AS MUCH FUN IN THEIR OWN ROOMS.

spoil your child rotten

...

WORSHIP YOUR MUSES:
Bonnie Cashin

Bonnie Cashin invented magenta. She lived in Northern California, loved a jewel tone, wrote poetry on her walls, and had a ball. She was also one of the most influential fashion designers of the '50s and '60s and liberated American sportswear from old-fashioned stuffiness. She hung around with other like-minded bon vivants and traveled and collected and created and lived a large life.

La Cashin's mantra was "Chic is where you find it." Her inspirations for clothing came more from poetry, literature, and music than from old frocks. The whimsy and wonder of everything she did is startling to me. I love her because she had a free spirit and a sense of play. As the world gets beige-er and beige-er, I strive to channel Bonnie Cashin's colorful spirit in everything I do.

THE ARTISANAL WEAVING TECHNIQUES
ADD EXTRA RICHNESS TO THESE CHEERY PINK AND
MAGENTA PILLOWS AND THROWS.

sometimes no color is the best color of all

In this store vignette, I gave myself the challenge of sticking to a rigid black-and-white color scheme. The result is glamorous and graphic. I spent an embarrassing number of hours lounging around on the sofa in various colored ensembles, using my outfit as an accent. A black-and-white backdrop makes people the stars of the room.

My Prescription For :
THE COLOR COMBO CLUELESS

3. REPLACE WHITE WALLS WITH **UNEXPECTED NEUTRALS** LIKE CAMEL, OLIVE, OR BABY BLUE.

1. THROW A DINNER PARTY AND **DYE ALL OF THE FOOD PURPLE.**

2. EBONIZE YOUR FLOORS. PALE WOOD FLOORS ARE A DRAG, AND PARQUET WOOD FLOORS ARE EVEN WORSE. **STAIN YOUR FLOORS** A DARK COLOR AND WATCH EVERY-THING IN THE ROOM COME TO LIFE.

4. LACQUER YOUR FRONT DOOR ORANGE. YOUR FRONT DOOR ANNOUNCES WHO YOU ARE, AND IT'S AN **IMPORTANT DETAIL** THAT MOST PEOPLE FORGET ABOUT. PIQUE YOUR NEIGHBORS' CURIOSITY.

5. USE UNEXPECTED TEXTURES ON YOUR WALLS TO TAKE COLOR TO A NEW LEVEL. A WALL UPHOLSTERED IN CHOCOLATE BROWN ULTRA-SUEDE IS HALSTON-IER THAN PLAIN OLD PAINT. USE GLOSSY PAINT FOR AN INSTANT **GLAMOUR INJECTION**. IF YOU'RE A CLEAN MODERNIST, TRY WHITE GRASS-CLOTH WALLPAPER FOR A LITTLE WARMTH.

7. HIDE A RIOT OF COLOR UNDER THE COVERS. YOU CAN BE RESTRAINED AND BUTTONED UP IN THE BEDROOM AND STILL **WILD BETWEEN THE SHEETS**. I LOVE SHEETS WITH BIG, BOLD FLORALS, PREPPY BAMBOO PATTERNS, AND JAUNTY STRIPES HIDDEN UNDER TAME COVERLETS.

8. BROWN AND BLUE. *MOI*'S SIGNATURE COLOR SCHEME IS THE ANSWER TO MOST OF YOUR PROBLEMS. **CHOCOLATE BROWN AND BABY BLUE** ARE PERFECT TOGETHER. THEY'RE UPTOWN AND DOWNTOWN, THEY'RE CLASSIC AND FASHION FORWARD, THEY'RE ME AND THEY'RE YOU. I DARE YOU TO THROW IN A LITTLE TAUPE AND SEE WHAT HAPPENS.

6. LEMON YELLOW. **LEMON YELLOW** IS THE ESSENCE OF CRISPNESS AND SHOULD NOT BE OVERLOOKED. ONE LEMON YELLOW PILLOW WILL INVIGORATE YOU MORE THAN A MILLION CUCUMBER MASKS.

...

LIBERATE YOUR INNER HIPPIE:

Organic Shapes and Earthy Colors

...

TAKE A TRIP TO BIG SUR

(if only in your mind)

My mother's friend Sylvia was a rich hippie poet who lived in Big Sur. (Thank God for inherited wealth.) Her house was incredible: It overlooked the sea and was all glass and raw beams, with a hot tub and outdoor shower. There was no plastic, no Tupperware, no wrinkle-free polyester sheets. Instead, there was string art, sculptures made by friends, a loom, and—I have come to suspect—lots and lots of drugs. She drove a 1967 Karmann Ghia and wore hand-embroidered caftans that were oddly compelling. To a Jewish suburban kid like myself, she always seemed sort of ethereal and far out, and I fantasized about one day growing up to be like her.

Today, I'm a potter. But to be honest with you, I'm about as un–hippie-dippy as you can get. I'm actually pretty bourgeois and conventional. I live in New York City and have a very un-potterish lifestyle. I'm addicted to *America's Next Top Model*. I read *Star* magazine every week. And I'm a huge devotee of the musical stylings of Justin Timberlake.

But a part of me still belongs to Birkenstocks and Bob Dylan, and that part of me comes out in my pottery. Because I live in an urban setting, I am completely deprived of any connection to the earth, so I try to make things that remind me of the organic forms, textures, and colors of Mother Nature. Most of us have to make a living in a conventional world and can't afford to tune in and drop out, but we can still have earthy, groovy homes.

recharge in a richly rustic retreat

Rustic modernism is the antidote for contemporary techno burnout. It's about wood, stone, craft, nubbly fabrics, and a hippie-go-lucky aesthetic. It's about closing your laptop and reading a book. It's about growing a garden instead of your 401(k). If you've become a cell-phone totin', email-answerin', brand identity–discussin', TiVO-lovin', multitaskin' mess, you need to embrace rustic hippie style.

BECAUSE THIS HOUSE IS PERCHED ON THE EDGE OF THE SEA, I WANTED TO MAKE THE ROOMS CONNECT TO THE LANDSCAPE OUTSIDE. IN THE LIVING ROOM, I USED GRASS CLOTH ON THE WALLS AND STRING DRAPES TO MATCH THE COLOR OF THE SAND. THE SLATE FLOORS MATCH THE COLOR OF THE SEA. OVERALL, THE ROOM HAS A DREAMY QUALITY, SO THAT IT'S HARD TO KNOW WHERE THE ROOM ENDS AND THE SEA BEGINS.

decorating can cure old psychological wounds

I was always incredibly jealous of my brother because he had a fun bedroom. He was lucky enough to have allergies and therefore had bachelor-ish cork floors instead of dreary old carpet. He had a TV in his room, and because he was a bit older, my parents thought that he could handle the responsibility of a hanging chair. He would torture me by never letting me swing in it.

Now I put hanging chairs everywhere. If you want to get in touch with your inner child, there's no need to read a hundred self-help books. Just hang a swing in your living room—you won't look back.

LIBERACE IS A SWINGER.

THE TEXTURES OF THIS ROOM ARE VERY RICH AND PEACEFUL, SO I WANTED THE FURNITURE TO BE THE STRONG, SILENT TYPE—GORGEOUS LINES AND MATERIALS, BUT QUIET AND HARMONIOUS. THE CHAIRS ARE BY GEORGE NAKASHIMA, THE RUG IS ANTIQUE MOROCCAN, AND THE CHEST IS BY WIDDICOMB FROM THE '50S. OF COURSE, I NEVER WANT A ROOM TO BE TOO QUIET, SO I ADDED THE BRIGHT ORANGE BACKGAMMON SET AND THE HAPPY OWL.

Nakashima chairs
+ Moroccan rug
+ flagstone wall
= Nirvana

...

THE LOUNGE AT THE PARKER IS VERY CHILL, AND IT'S WHERE EVERYONE WANTS TO BE. THE ROOM IS BUILT AROUND A CENTRAL FIREPLACE THAT'S ALMOST AS COMPELLING AS TV. ONE OF MY FAVORITE THINGS ABOUT THE HOTEL IS THAT IT'S VERY DOG-FRIENDLY. THERE ARE ALWAYS A FEW PUPS LOUNGING NEAR THE FIRE, AND IT FEELS LIKE HOME.

beware: a round fireplace in your living room will guarantee lots of visitors

91

A FEW YEARS AGO, I VISITED THE BRIGHTON PAVILION IN BRIGHTON, ENGLAND, AND IT BLEW MY MIND. PLUNKED DOWN IN THE MIDDLE OF SOGGY *ANGLETERRE* IS A CHINOISE FANTASY BUILT, IN THE LATE 18TH CENTURY, AS A SELF-INDULGENT ESCAPE BY THE PRINCE REGENT GEORGE IV. IN THE 1960S AND '70S, THE SPIRIT OF THE BRIGHTON PAVILION WAS KEPT ALIVE BY THE HOLLWOOD DECORATOR TONY DUQUETTE, WHO FAMOUSLY PROCLAIMED THAT ONE SHOULD "LEAVE NO SURFACE UNDECORATED." DUQUETTE'S INTERIORS, WITH THEIR FUSION OF MODERNISM AND EXOTICISM, MADE HIS HOLLYWOOD CLIENTS SEEM MORE INTERESTING THAN THEY PROBABLY WERE. THE POOL AT THE PARKER WANTED A LITTLE *QUELQUE CHOSE D'AUTRE*, SO I, ALONG WITH LANDSCAPE ARCHITECT JUDY KAMEON, CHANNELED THE PRINCE REGENT AND LA DUQUETTE AND PUNCTUATED THE DESERT LANDSCAPE WITH A BALINESE FOLLY.

IF YOU WANT TO BE A RICH HIPPIE BUT AREN'T
A) RICH OR B) A HIPPIE, TRY THE FOLLOWING:
MAKE SOME SUN TEA. READ *TROPIC OF CANCER* OR
THE DHARMA BUMS. FORGET ABOUT THE SOUTH
BEACH DIET AND SPRINKLE WHEAT GERM ON EVERY-
THING YOU EAT. CHANGE YOUR NAME TO CINNAMON.
LISTEN TO JONI MITCHELL WHILE YOU TAKE UP
GLASSBLOWING.

make pots, not war

let the sun shine in

Norma's, one of the restaurants at the Parker, is the sunniest, nicest place to eat breakfast in the world. The shell is earthy and organic—white brick walls, a warm wood floor, and leather chairs—but it called out for a layer of sweetness. So, I made a series of sun plaques for the walls. The vase on the table is also a sun, the placemats are crewel-work flowers, and the salt and pepper shakers are little birds. Your breakfast room should make you smile.

get crafty

This is a ceramic tile frieze that I made for the concierge desk at the Parker. It's a montage depicting the giggly fun that guests can expect to have at the hotel, beginning with a groovy couple arriving in their Jaguar for a sun-filled weekend by the pool. I incorporated words ("Eat, drink, and be merry, for tomorrow you shall check out") and embossed symbols of some of my favorite hedonistic things: diamonds, dollar bills, and valium. The oversize key hanging on the wall is from 19th-century England and used to hang in a locksmith's shop. I love the idea of an old-fashioned key in this era of hotel key cards.

IT'S OK TO BE SENTIMENTAL. THE PICTURE OVER THE BED IN THIS PARKER GUESTROOM IS A WATERCOLOR BY RUBEN TOLEDO OF HIS WIFE, ISABEL. HE LOVES, LOVES, *LOVES* HIS WIFE, AND IT REALLY COMES THROUGH IN HIS INCREDIBLE ARTWORK. THE SURFACES IN THIS ROOM ARE LUXURIOUS AND ORGANIC: THE FLOOR IS SISAL, THE CEILING IS COVERED IN GRASS CLOTH, THE HAND-THROWN LAMPS HAVE STRING SHADES. ALL OF THESE ELEMENTS ARE JUXTAPOSED WITH THE RIGID MINIMALIST BED. BUT THE FINAL AND BEST LAYER COMES FROM TOLEDO'S PORTRAIT; IT ADDS FEELINGS OF WARMTH AND LOVE THAT REALLY MAKE THE ROOM. **OPPOSITE PAGE:** GRASS, PUPPIES, AND MOONBEAMS—THESE ARE A FEW OF MY FAVORITE THINGS. (BUT NOTE THAT "CASH" TAKES CENTER STAGE.)

tickle your senses with
tantalizing textures

center yourself with raw beams, olive walls, and low light

FOR THE GUEST ROOM IN OUR SHELTER ISLAND HOUSE, WE WENT WITH A MORE EARTHY COLOR PALETTE, THINKING THAT OUR GUESTS MIGHT NEED A REPRIEVE FROM THE SCREAMING COLORS OF THE REST OF THE HOUSE. THE NUDE PAINTING IS BY MY LATE FATHER. HE WAS A LAWYER WHO SPENT EVERY SPARE MOMENT IN HIS BASEMENT PAINT-ING AND SCULPTURE STUDIO. ART FOR HIM WASN'T A VEHICLE FOR CAREER SUCCESS OR VALIDATION. HE MADE STUFF BECAUSE HE TRULY LOVED TO. SOMETIMES, WHEN I AM IN THE MIDDLE OF A GRUELING DAY RUNNING MY MINI-EMPIRE, I THINK HE WAS VERY WISE TO HAVE STAYED IN THE BASE-MENT, HAPPILY MAKING HIS ART.

Reform Synagogue Architecture

I WANTED MY REFORM TEMPLE VASES TO BE LIKE A JAZZ COMPOSITION: THE ANGLES INTERACT WITH EACH OTHER IN AN IMPROBABLE AND INTUITIVE WAY. THE INSET FORMS PLAY OFF THE COMPOSITION, WHILE THE TEXTURES—SHINY AND MATTE, SMOOTH AND GROOVED—ADD ANOTHER LAYER TO THE HEADY MIX.

Italy Schmitaly. If you want to see sublime sanctuaries, forget about the Vatican—just get in your car and head over to your local Reform temple.

Places of worship have always been over the top. Communities open their handbags wide to show their commitment to God, and they give architects free rein to create transcendental shrines. And, to me, Reform temples are the transcendental-est.

Reform temples thumb their noses at the traditions of architecture. They say goodbye to straight lines and hello to curves. They bid *adieu* to rigid thinking and *bonjour* to new ideas. For me, they take synagogue attendance from *je ne veux pas* to *je ne sais quoi*.

The reckless disregard for convention evident in Reform temples is completely liberating to me. When I'm feeling constricted by pottery dogma (pots should be round, mugs need handles, etc.), I think of the organic, rule-breaking forms of Temple Israel in Miami or Temple Beth-El in Great Neck, and I feel inspired.

107

LET NATURE TAKE CENTER STAGE. WE USED
NO WINDOW TREATMENTS IN OUR SHELTER ISLAND
HOME SO THAT WE COULD FEEL CONNECTED TO
THE TREES OUTSIDE. THE HOUSE IS RUSTIC, SO WIN-
DOW TREATMENTS WOULD HAVE SEEMED FRUMPY.
WHY BOTHER SPENDING WEEKENDS IN THE COUNTRY
IF YOU DON'T LOVE THE VIEW?

THIS PAGE: IN THE LIVING ROOM OF THIS BROOKLYN BROWNSTONE, I USED SOFT LIGHT, QUIET COLORS, AND SYMMETRICAL ARRANGEMENTS TO CREATE A SENSE OF ORDER AND PEACE. WHEN YOU WALK IN, YOU FEEL LIKE YOU'RE LEAVING THE CHAOS OF THE URBAN WORLD BEHIND YOU. **OPPOSITE PAGE:** THIS TOWN-HOUSE HAS VERY GRAND ARCHITECTURE, BUT THE OWNERS ARE YOUNG MODERNS WHO WANTED IT TO FEEL CASUAL. A CHOREOGRAPHED DISARRAY CAN MAKE PEOPLE FEEL AT HOME.

My Prescription For :
BOHEMIAN BLISS

1. TAKE **TAMBOURINE** LESSONS.

2. COLLECT VINTAGE *SUNSET* BOOKS (WWW.ALIBRIS. COM). *SUNSET* MAGAZINE HAS ALWAYS CAPTURED THE OPTIMISM OF CALIFORNIA LIFE, AND THESE COMPREHENSIVE BOOKS ARE ESSENTIAL REFERENCE TOOLS FOR **RUSTIC MODERN LIVING**. MY TWO FAVES ARE *WALKS, WALLS & PATIO FLOORS* AND *CABINS & VACATION HOUSES*.

3. WALLPAPER YOUR BED-ROOM CEILING WITH GRASS CLOTH. **NATURAL MATERIALS** WILL SET YOU FREE.

4. DRINK YOUR MORN-ING COFFEE OUT OF A HAND-THROWN MUG. TAKE OFF YOUR PRADA HEELS AND PUT YOUR FEET ON A MOROCCAN LEATHER HASSOCK. **STRUM A GUITAR** INSTEAD OF WRITING AN E-MAIL. SLOW DOWN AND ENJOY YOUR LIFE.

5. SUZANIS, SUZANIS, SUZANIS. THESE UZBEKSTANI WEDDING SHAWLS ARE DE RIGUEUR FOR **BOHEMIAN BONA FIDES.** SUZANIS ARE ORNATE AND ETHNIC AND GORGEOUS AND MAKE FANTASTIC DRAPES OR SOFA COVERS. VISIT WWW.SUZANIS.COM TO SEE OODLES OF THESE GORGEOUS TAPESTRIES.

7. THROW OUT YOUR BLACKBERRY AND GO PICK SOME **ACTUAL BLACKBERRIES.**

8. **GO BAREFOOT.** TITILLATE YOUR TOES WITH SISAL AND PAMPER YOUR PAWS WITH FURRY SHEEPSKIN RUGS. SURROUND YOURSELF WITH NATURAL TEXTURES—YOUR HOME SHOULD FEEL AS GOOD AS IT LOOKS.

6. GO BACK TO SCHOOL TO **BECOME A VETERINARIAN.** LET'S FACE IT, THAT REGIONAL SALES MEETING REALLY ISN'T ALL THAT IMPORTANT IN THE SCHEME OF THINGS.

HANDCRAFTED TCHOTCHKES ARE LIFE-ENHANCING:

Layer Your Lair With Love

· · ·

LOVE
WHAT YOU
LOVE

Every object in your house should have a raison d'être and be meaningful to you. So often, the homes featured in upscale design magazines seem to be covered in a beige haze of graciousness. Everything is something-"esque:" an African-esque this, a Tuscan-esque that, all trying to create a "personal-esque" atmosphere. Obviously, it's all stuff picked out by the decorator. One gets the feeling that even the pictures in the picture frames are of beautiful strangers.

People who push bland, soulless decorative objects on you have blood on their hands. You know how the government subsidizes farmers not to grow too much corn to avoid surplus? I think that the government should get involved and do the same thing with members of the gift community who are filling people's homes with moderate, lifeless tchotchkes. If you do find yourself coerced into buying these objects, I suggest making the shipping address your local thrift store, or having them shipped directly to the back corners of your garage, where they won't be able to depress you.

I think that you should surround yourself with objects that are personal. When you furnish your home, you should buy what you love rather than ponder what the Smiths down the block might think. The more eccentric your choices, the better.

I live for unusual bits and bobs. I haunt thrift stores in search of giant fiber-art balls of yarn, collages of vintage cars made from antique watch parts, or burlap busts of George Washington. I am drawn to designers who have unique styles, like Fornasetti, Bjorn Wiinblad, and Rei Kawakubo. As a designer myself, I follow my heart and make the stuff that I want rather than following trends. When I make a giant porcelain vase covered in breasts, I take a leap of faith that others will enjoy my personal vision. I love to make things, and I hope it shows.

accessorize with aplomb

Most people stop decorating too soon. Once you have the walls and floors and furniture in place, it's the finishing touches that can really take a room from *ordinaire* to *extraordinaire*: collections of favorite objects, art on the walls (or the doors or the banister of your staircase), over-the-top drapery and window treatments, or giant chandeliers hung above it all. These are the details that take you from like to love, from complacency to ecstasy.

allergic to fur?
adopt a
ceramic pet
instead
...

THIS PAGE: THE FOYER IN THIS NEW YORK APARTMENT IS GRACIOUS AND TRADITIONAL, WITH FANCY WALLPAPER AND MIRRORED DOORS. BUT TO KEEP IT FROM SEEMING TOO GROWN-UP, I ADDED THE FLOWER-SHAPED LIGHT FIXTURE. A SINGLE MOD GESTURE—A GRAPHIC PILLOW, AN ORANGE LAMP, A PACO RABANNE FROCK—CAN MAKE AN OLD ROOM FEEL YOUNG AND PLAYFUL. **OPPOSITE PAGE:** CENTERPIECES ARE ALWAYS A BIT VEXING. A BASKET OF DRIED FLOWERS? YAWN. FRUIT BOWL? FRUIT-FLY MAGNET. CANDELABRA? FUNEREAL. THE ANSWER TO THE AGE-OLD CENTER-PIECE CONUNDRUM IS CERAMIC ANIMALS. THIS ZEBRA OWNS THE TABLETOP AND GIVES YOUR EYE A PLACE TO FOCUS.

gift-giving and portraiture

Simon and I both work in the world of stuff, and at some point in our relationship it became impossible to think of yet another thing to give each other when gift-giving occasions arose. One year, I took the advice of many women's magazines and made him a coupon book of personal services that he could redeem throughout the year: one hour of classical music on the home stereo (when I was not there); one veto of a *Law and Order* episode (not redeemable until rerun season); a coupon for a one-month stay at the Personality Improvement Center, etc. Much to my surprise, my husband did not appreciate my thoughtful gift, and I had to pick up the pieces and move on.

I finally found the perfect gift: portraits. It started innocently enough, when I commissioned a painting of us with our dog, Liberace. Simon loved it. Portraiture is a tradition that's sadly fallen off. Portraits play into the narcissism of birthdays and holidays. Why hang pictures in your house of other people ("Girl with Fruit and Sheaves of Wheat")? Why not hang art of yourself and your loved ones?

My portraiture obsession has now developed into a quest for increasingly deranged mediums: silhouettes of our profiles; cursive handwriting of our names covering an entire page; putting each other's faces on birthday cakes. Be narcissistic: Put a picture of yourself on the wall.

JONATHAN

is in the gift community

SIMON

Lied about his height
on his passport

just because clowns are creepy doesn't mean you shouldn't put one over your fireplace.

kitsch: discriminate but don't dismiss

Once, at a thrift store in Palm Beach, a poodle lamp caught my eye. It was so Vegas that, in spite of my fondness for dogs, I thought I couldn't possibly put it in my home—too kitschy. But when I considered its majestic scale and gorgeous coat, I saw that I couldn't say no. Today, the poodle proudly presides over my New York bedroom.

In general, I don't like kitsch. Pink flamingoes on the front lawn? Thanks, but no. But I do like kitsch when it's married to craft, when it's idiosyncratic and beautifully made. I live to hunt for amusing pieces, and inevitably it's the things in questionable taste—inappropriate, vulgar, or a little kooky—that make a room memorable. Diana Vreeland once said, "A little bad taste is like a nice splash of paprika. No taste is what I'm against."

THIS PAGE, TOP: MARQUETRY, THE ART OF WOOD INLAID IN ELABORATE PATTERNS, IS ONE OF THE GREAT CRAFTS OF ITALY. SADLY, MARQUETRY ARTISANS NOW CRAFT DREARY PASTORAL SCENES, BUT SIMON AND I FOUND THESE '70S CLOWNS AT THE BOTTOM OF A DUSTY SHELF IN CAPRI AND RESCUED THEM FROM OBLIVION. BOTTOM: I COLLECT A REALLY WEIRD GENRE OF ART, WHICH IS VINTAGE CAR ASSEMBLAGES MADE FROM OLD WATCH PARTS AND HARDWARE.

129

THE PROVENANCE OF OUR FUNKSTER ARTWORK VARIES WIDELY, BUT IT'S ALL EQUALLY BELOVED. WE FOUND THE MICHAEL JACKSON BUST AT A FLEA MARKET FOR $20. THE LUCITE PORTRAITS OF GEORGE CLINTON AND JIMI HENDRIX ARE BY A FOLK ARTIST NAMED STEVE CALIGURI. AND PRINCE'S HEAD WAS MADE BY MARTHA KING FOR A BARNEYS WINDOW.

funkify your life

Recently, Simon and I surveyed our New York pad and thought smugly, "This apartment is a three-dimensional expression of who we are as people, and the art choices are perfect. Could we be more brilliant?" Then, as we looked around, we realized that all of the art featured funk icons or hetero soft-core porn.

Helen Keller could see that we are neither R&B musicians nor porn stars. The truth is, we are more like a couple of herbal tea–sipping grandmothers. We are blissfully content but rather vanilla: We don't drink, and we're in bed by ten. Whence the art?

Your stuff (art, *objets*, furniture) can reflect sides of your personality that rarely see the light of day. Clearly, our idiosyncratic, if not louche, collections provide Simon and me with much-needed vicarious outlets. (And, for the record, I think you'd be better off expressing your bad-ass side with art rather than a midlife tattoo. Tattoos are like permanent bell-bottoms.)

IN THIS NEW YORK LIVING ROOM, I TREATED THE FLAT-SCREEN TV AND THE TORTOISE-FINISH LAMPSHADE LIKE PIECES OF ART AND USED THEM AS COMPOSITIONAL ELEMENTS IN THE ARRANGEMENT.

do it salon-style

Hanging art might seem intimidating, but it is actually quite simple. Be intuitive—hang a large picture first and then just keep on going. One principle I like to follow is to ignore the content of the art and think of the pictures as geometric forms that need to be composed nicely, almost like a Mondrian painting. Ignore moldings, hang things on bookshelves, and be casual.

arrange with attitude

People often think that the ability to arrange things well is a gift that some have and some don't. But I've learned that the key to good arrangements is experimenting. You just have to start. When arranging objects on a shelf, try whatever pops into your head, and eventually you'll get good at it. Try symmetry, or groups of three objects at different heights, or tight clusters of objects with space around them. The most important thing is that the objects you choose be things you love to look at.

put flowers in an umbrella stand and ostrich feathers in a candle holder

THIS PAGE: IN THE LOBBY OF THE PARKER, WE NEEDED AN EXTRA LAYER OF ZSOOSH, SO I USED AN OLD '70S TRICK—THROWING A BIG CLUSTER OF OSTRICH FEATHERS INTO A CANDLE HOLDER. IT'S THEATRICAL, IT'S CAMP, IT'S OF QUESTIONABLE TASTE, AND I LOVE IT. **OPPOSITE PAGE:** I LIKE TO MIX RICH, FANCY TEXTURES WITH PLAYFUL POP ICONOGRAPHY. THE WALLS IN OUR NEW YORK CITY FOYER ARE A COLLAGE BY THE ARTIST JEAN-PAUL PHILIPPE MADE OF LAYERS OF WHITEWASHED BURLAP. THE AREA REALLY COMES TO LIFE WITH THE ADDITION OF A '70S LUCITE CHAIR, A NEEDLEPOINT PILLOW OF LIZA MINNELLI, AND A GIANT FORNASETTI FOOT. THE PHOTOGRAPH ON THE WALL IS A SELF-PORTRAIT OF CINDY SHERMAN DRESSED AS A SCARY MONSTER RUNNING THROUGH THE WOODS IN A RED GINGHAM OUTFIT. IT'S THE FIRST THING WE SEE WHEN WE WALK IN THE DOOR.

divine drapery

I grew up in a modern house, so I'm a recent convert to the draped lifestyle. And like most recent converts, I'm very zealous in my devotion. Nothing takes a room from drab to deluxe like floor-to-ceiling drapes. There was a time in American decorating when every house had some over-the-top drapery treatment with some completely koo-koo valance. Sadly, that time has passed, and people have embraced pared-down window treatments, if any at all. I say, Stop! Turn back the hands of time! I love to peruse '60s home decorating books for improbable drapery ideas. You can do a heraldic valance with a nailhead trim; a roman shade with a taped ribbon border; or simply patch two pieces of fabric together. With drapery, anything goes. Also, as eclecticism has taken over the world of decorating, I think people are forgetting the majesty of matching your drapes to your bedspread or sofa. Sometimes the most obvious solution is the most triumphant.

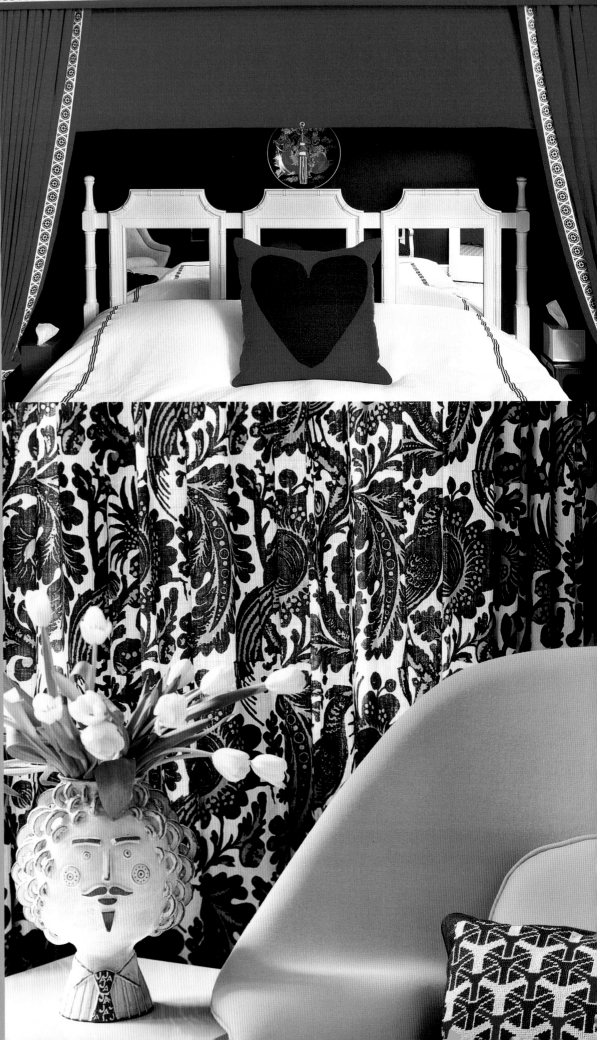

My Prescription For :
FILLING YOUR HOME WITH THINGS YOU LOVE

1. PUT A TV IN EVERY ROOM IN YOUR HOME. **LOTS AND LOTS** OF TVS. EVERYWHERE.

2. LIBERATE YOURSELF FROM THE SHACKLES OF PROVENANCE. IF YOU LOVE AN IMAGE IN A BOOK, TEAR IT OUT AND PUT IT IN A FANCY FRAME. **MY FAVORITE SOURCES** FOR FRAMEABLE *TROUVÉS* ARE THE 1973 PIRELLI CALENDAR WITH ALLEN JONES'S KINKY GIRLS OR *THE PHOTOGRAPHS OF RON GALELLA*.

3. START A **COLLECTION**: CERAMIC ANIMALS, MANNEQUIN HEADS, OTHER PEOPLE'S HIGH SCHOOL YEARBOOKS.

4. EMBRACE ECCLESI-ASTICAL PARAPHERNALIA FROM THE '60S. AS MOST DESIGN HAS BECOME DREARY, ECCLESIASTICAL SUP-PLIES (CANDLE HOLDERS, CHALICES, BOXES) HAVE MAINTAINED A '60S **GO-GO LOOK**. I FIRST DISCOVERED THIS GENRE WHEN I WAS IN ROME AND STUMBLED INTO A CHURCH SUPPLIES STORE—EVERYTHING LOOKED LIKE IT WAS MADE BY A DANISH CRAFTSMAN. GO STRAIGHT TO ROME OR VISIT WWW.CHURCH-SUPPLIES.COM.

5. MAKE STUFF. LEARN TO BLOW GLASS, NEEDLEPOINT A BELT FOR YOUR HUSBAND, MAKE A MACRAMÉ OWL. IT'S MUCH MORE **EXCITING** TO MAKE SOMETHING THAN TO BUY SOMETHING. YOU COULD EVEN TAKE A POTTERY CLASS—JUST DON'T PUT ME OUT OF BUSINESS.

6. SPEND **ALL DAY SURFING** EBAY INSTEAD OF WORKING. (OH WAIT, YOU ALREADY DO THAT.) SOME OF MY FAVORITE SEARCHES ARE EAMES, C. JERE, RAYMOR, RISOM, WEGNER, WORMLEY, PAUL EVANS, KARL SPRINGER, PARZINGER, GIBBINGS, JUHL, PLATNER, MURANO, SPUTNIK, AND ARTELUCE.

7. REARRANGE YOUR FURNITURE. THERE'S NEVER ONE SINGLE ANSWER FOR A FURNITURE LAYOUT, SO KEEP PLAYING AND **TRYING NEW THINGS.** A NEW ARRANGEMENT CAN BE AN INSTANT FACELIFT FOR YOUR HOUSE AND MAKE EVERYTHING SEEM FRESH. PLUS, IT BURNS LOTS OF CALORIES.

8. STOCK YOUR GUEST ROOM WITH **BOOKS** THAT PEOPLE WILL ACTUALLY WANT TO READ: *VALLEY OF THE DOLLS, SCRUPLES, SEX AND THE SINGLE GIRL.*

...

PALM BEACH
CHIC:

Classical Lines and Shiny Surfaces, with a
Top Note of Cinematic Glamour

PALM BEACH
through the eyes of
a jewish potter

On my first day of high school, I wore the same outfit that I always wore to Friday night synagogue services: gray suit pants, a crisp white shirt, a navy blazer, and a clip-on tie. Unfortunately, my first day of high school occurred in 1980 in an incredibly preppy, WASPy place: Wilmington, Delaware, a town riddled with DuPont heirs and exclusive cotillions. Needless to say, I was ostracized and forced to share a locker with my fellow raging dork, Steve T.

I wanted desperately to fit in but didn't know how. Then, in walked Timothy Weymouth, wearing ratty Levi's cords, Clarks Wallabees held together with duct tape, his father's hand-me-down button-down shirt with a Lacoste shirt under it, and a whale-embroidered belt. Everything he wore looked as if it had been run over by the family's Jeep Wagoneer during a ski trip to Vermont.

I quickly came to learn that Wilmington WASP culture was about unrelenting efforts to look like you didn't care about anything and were down to your last dime. I imagined that this laissez-faire attitude was an affectation, and that they really lived in glamorous splendor in the privacy of their own homes. But, when I finally got invited into their homes, I was horrified to see how they actually lived: Everything looked old, run-down, and, on top of it all, uncomfortable.

As it turns out, there are two kinds of WASPs: real WASPs and the WASPs of my imagination. I was looking for Katharine Hepburn in *The Philadelphia Story*, while the WASPs around me were wearing third-hand clothes. So where were the glamorous aristocratic WASPs I had dreamed about? The answer is that they were all in Palm Beach.

In Palm Beach, WASPs know how to be WASPs. Think cheerful needlepoint message pillows, monogrammed everything, snobbism, and Lilly, Lilly, Lilly. Palm Beach WASPs belong to exclusive country clubs, have servants and fancy cars, and spend their money. Timothy Weymouth needs to get on a plane (first class—he can afford it!), head to Palm Beach, and see how he should be living his life.

In the meantime, this Jew has a mission: to inflict Palm Beach WASPy grandeur on the homes of America, one needlepoint pillow at a time.

live out your delusions of grandeur

When you were little, you probably imagined that someday you would live in a grand manner: a castle, a mansion, an elegant duplex at the very least. Now you've settled for moderate surroundings, practical solutions, and compromise. How utterly realistic and dreary! Why shouldn't you be grand in your own home?

Palm Beach style provides an immediate transfusion of luxury, glamour, and elegance into your veins. For me, it's about making traditional elements bold and young. It's about indulging in fantasy and forgetting about reality. Make your home as luxe as your wildest imaginings allow. Think too highly of yourself. Does it really hurt?

go outside and play

For the Parker croquet lawn, I found some rusty old lawn furniture at a thrift shop (I call this style Mexican Rococo), painted it white, and upholstered the cushions in bright green Sunbrella outdoor fabric with contrasting white piping. I highly recommend taking up croquet—it'll make you feel like you're living in a Merchant Ivory movie.

don't have a lawn? buy two fiberglass foo dogs for your balcony

These giant beauties look like they're made of stone and should probably crash through the balcony of our Palm Beach apartment and land on poor old Mrs. Rosenbloom below. But—surprise—they're actually fiberglass and only weigh about 50 pounds each. We found them in Chinatown outside of a restaurant that was going out of business. These foo dogs add instant glamour to our small balcony. (I just hope that they don't blow away during hurricane season and crush Mrs. Rosenbloom after all.)

150

MY LIVING ROOM IN NEW YORK HAS VERY GRAND ARCHITECTURE, A VAULTED CEILING, AND ELABORATE MOLDINGS. BUT THE LIGHTING SOLUTION TURNED OUT NOT TO BE SO FANCY: STYROFOAM CUPS. I REPRISED AN OLD DECORATING TRICK OF MY MOTHER'S BY GLUING TOGETHER STYROFOAM CUPS TO MAKE GIANT GLOBES THAT WORK PERFECTLY IN THE SOARING SPACE.

CLOCKWISE FROM TOP LEFT: MURANO GLASS CHANDELIERS ADD TWINKLE AND ELEGANCE TO ANY ROOM. A GIANT FLOWER CEILING FIXTURE RULES OVER A SMALL SPACE AND LOOKS AWESOME. THIS TWELVE-FOOT-HIGH CHANDELIER HANGS IN THE LOBBY OF THE PARKER AND IS MADE FROM 1,500 INDIVIDUAL PIECES OF GLASS STRUNG TOGETHER; IT ORIGINALLY HUNG IN A SUBLIME PALM BEACH ESTATE CALLED "LA RONDA," WHICH WAS DESTROYED TO MAKE ROOM FOR A MCMANSION. (I'M DREADING HAVING TO CHANGE A LIGHT BULB.) BUY SPUTNIK-SHAPED FIXTURES AND USE GIANT BULBS. A PISTILLO LIGHT, NAMED FOR THE PISTILS OF A FLOWER, MAKES A STAID ROOM FEEL GO-GO.

be a size queen when it comes to chandeliers

Chandeliers are a sublime opportunity for immodesty, and I'm obsessed with them. Chandeliers should always be a little bit bigger than you imagined, a little bit glitzier than you're comfortable with, and a little bit more expensive than you can afford. I especially love vintage chandeliers—the more over-the-top the better. I like to use large, oversize bulbs in them. My philosophy is: Don't be tentative when it comes to choosing a chandelier.

153

mad for
mantiques

I interrupt this essay to issue a command: Put down this book, run to your nearest video store, and rent *X Y & Zee*, a 1972 movie starring Elizabeth Taylor and Michael Caine. This seminal movie about the dissolution of a swinging marriage makes *Who's Afraid of Virginia Woolf?* (another movie in which Elizabeth Taylor brays at her husband) seem like child's play. The film bristles with electricity and, more importantly for this book, bristles with what I have come to call "mantiques." What are mantiques, you ask?

Michael Caine and Elizabeth Taylor have separate bedrooms. Hers is ultra feminine and features a floor-model hair dryer. His is archetypically masculine, and it looks divine. Why does style have to be democratic? Virginia Woolf wrote that every woman needs a room of her own. But bit by bit, women have taken over the home decorating world and put their imprimatur on the entire house. I think it's time for men to take back the night, at least in a small way. The perfect place to do that is in the den, where every man should have a comfy and masculine place to hang out, filled with mantiques: suits of armor, leather Chesterfield sofas, brass valets, shades of brown and red, and dark wood paneling with erotic pop art on top of it. Ultimately, it's where the women will want to hang out, too.

155

butch it up

This is the interior of Mr. Parker's, the restaurant at the Parker. We created a fictitious muse called Mrs. Parker—sort of an inspirational Auntie Mame type—and imagined the hotel as her incredible estate: residential, eclectic, and fun. We imagined that Mrs. Parker has a husband, a dissolute philanderer called Mr. Parker, and that this is his lair. As a backdrop, we created a wood-paneled masculine hideaway and then added a mixture of gothic and mod appointments. The final and most important layer is Mr. Parker's art collection, which consists of lots of racy, erotic pop art, hung salon-style. The restaurant is an improbable mix of gothic and mod, and being there makes me feel groovier than I actually am.

tassels are the earrings of the home

Until recently, I felt about tassels the same as I felt about the color teal—I hated them! Tassels seemed fusty and depressing and *Designing Women*-ish. But there is a thin line between love and hate, and my passionate hatred for tassels could only mean one thing: I was about to fall in love with them.

Sure enough, they started to look really good to me, and now I use them everywhere to add extra flair. Dreary lampshade? Tassel. Blah doorknob? Tassel. Uninspired drapes? Tassel fringe.

I've always thought that earrings serve an incredible function: They make boring old ears seem special and sensual. Tassels are the earrings of the home.

OPPOSITE PAGE: MAKE YOUR FOYER GREAT. IT'S THE FIRST PLACE YOU SEE WHEN YOU COME HOME AT THE END OF THE DAY AND THE LAST PLACE YOU SEE AS YOU BID YOUR HOME ADIEU AND SAIL OUT INTO THE WORLD. LET YOUR FOYER SAY "HELLO!" AND "COME BACK SOON!" I LIKE TO TAKE TRADITIONAL (AND USEFUL) ELEMENTS LIKE UMBRELLA HOLDERS AND HAT STANDS AND TWEAK THEM TO MAKE THEM FUN AND HAPPY. EVERYONE NEEDS A PLACE TO PUT UMBRELLAS; WHY NOT MAKE THE UMBRELLA HOLDER A GIANT OWL? THIS FOYER HAS TRADITIONAL ELEMENTS—CHINOISERIE-INSPIRED WALLPAPER, A QUEEN ANNE BENCH—BUT I KEPT THE COLOR SCHEME RESTRAINED TO MAKE IT FEEL GRAPHIC AND MODERN.

OPPOSITE PAGE: EVERY GIRL NEEDS A PERCH TO SORT THROUGH INVITATIONS AND THANK-YOU NOTES.

give in to high-gloss glamour

Playlist

DRINK: VODKA GIMLETS

WEAR: GOBS OF KENNETH JAY LANE COSTUME JEWELRY

WATCH: *THE GALLOPING GOURMET*

EAT: YOUR SECOND DESSERT

add some zest to your nest

This kitchen is incredibly luxe, with all of the expected bells and whistles—a marble this and a Sub-Zero that. I went with a very traditional fabric, but in a bright orange to make the kitchen young and fun. My favorite touches are the chairs by design icon Norman Cherner, which I tweaked with a coat of white lacquer and brocade print fabric. Then I added lampshades and banquettes to match. Traditionalia doesn't have to be tame.

165

THIS PAGE: PATTERNED WALLPAPER ALLOWS SOLID, BOLD SHAPES TO REALLY POP. USING DECORATIVE TRIM ON THE LAMPSHADE AND WINDOW TREATMENT PULLS THE WHOLE LOOK TOGETHER. IF TASSELS ARE THE EARRINGS OF THE HOME, DECORATIVE TRIM IS THE NECKLACE. **OPPSITE PAGE:** I LOVE TO USE CLASSIC, UPTOWN MOTIFS—HOUNDSTOOTH, GREEK KEY, CANING—RENDERED IN DOWNTOWN, CRAFTY FABRICATIONS, LIKE THIS HAND-LOOMED LLAMA RUG.

count sheep like a contessa

. . .

WORSHIP YOUR MUSES:
SLIM AARONS

Slim Aarons' book *A Wonderful Time* documents the fashions, homes, and lifestyles of America's aristocracy in the '50s, '60s, and '70s. It is my bible.

Outsiders can often understand cultures to which they don't belong better than natives. One of my favorite directors is Douglas Sirk, whose movies are both a celebration and a critique of postwar American material excess and optimism. He was born in Switzerland, but he understood America as only a foreigner could. His is a fetishistic but loving and incredibly illuminating perspective.

With the same outsider's eye, Slim Aarons captured the life and style of America's elite. His pictures are optimistic, excessive, glamorous, and appreciative. I'm sure his subjects had complicated lives, but you'd never know it from his pictures. Interiors are over the top, money abounds, fashion is chic, and life is fun. None of the lives he chronicles are moderate. In my decorating, I always hope that my clients will look back on the homes I helped them create and think of all the happy times in their lives. And, at the risk of sounding overly sincere, I hope that you, *cher readeur*, make your homes playful and glamorous settings. Look good, live well, and take lots and lots of pictures.

171

HOLLYWOOD LIFE
Eliot Elisofon

Ellsworth Kelly FONDATION BEYELER

Bill Blass AN AMERICAN DESIGNER

Allure Diana Vreeland BULFINCH

TROVA

DESIGNERS' OWN HOMES ARCHITECTURAL DIGEST

Louis Kahn
Dahl-Wolfe

MARIMEKKO

SO80S
PATRICK McMULLAN

live happily ever after

Palm Beach chic is a state of mind. This apartment is in New York, but stepping inside feels like going on a mini-vacation. The colors are bright and happy, the feeling is cozy, and the little lady on the coffee table is always there to say *bienvenue*. The lady of the house (the owner, not the vase) grew up in Palm Beach in a house in which everything matched, and she wanted to re-create that spirit. So, I used the same yellow trim everywhere, while the green crewel fabric shows up in some unexpected places—on bands at the top and bottom of the drapes and on the throw pillows. The big brown chairs add a layer of gravitas (if you ignore the playful trim), and the platinum lamps and Lucite accessories add twinkle.

173

My Prescription For :
DELUXE DELIRIUM

1. CARRY A SQUASH RACQUET EVERYWHERE FOR INSTANT **OLD-MONEY CRED**.

2. IF I'VE SAID IT ONCE, I'VE SAID IT A THOUSAND TIMES: **MATCH EVERYTHING.** CHOOSE ONE FABRIC AND USE IT CONSTANTLY—UPHOLSTERED WALLS, MATCHING DRAPES, SOFAS, CHAIRS, THROW PILLOWS, PANTSUITS. SOMETIMES THE SIMPLEST SOLUTION IS THE BEST.

3. BUY RICH LADIES' SCARVES AND MAKE THEM INTO PILLOWS. SEARCH EBAY FOR ONES BY VERA, CARDIN, HERMÈS, OR DIOR.

4. NAME YOUR HOUSE AFTER AN ENGLISH COUNTRY ESTATE—BALMORAL ARMS, SANDRINGHAM, BLENHEIM—AND HAVE THE NAME IMPRINTED ON MATCHBOOKS, NAPKINS, AND STATIONERY (WWW.SUN-RISE.COM). THIS IS AN ESPECIALLY GOOD IDEA IF YOU LIVE IN A STUDIO APARTMENT OR A SUBURB OF BUFFALO. **TONGUE-IN-CHEEK GRANDIOSITY** IS GOOD FOR THE SOUL.

5. SURRENDER TO THE POWER OF LIME GREEN. LIME AND CHOCOLATE, LIME AND PINK, LIME AND WHITE, LIME AND YOU. LIME IS CRISP AND CLARIFYING AND OPTIMISTIC. THERE'S A REASON WHY WASPS THROW IT IN THEIR GIN AND TONICS.

6. PUT REGAL FURNITURE IN YOUR BATHROOM. STACK YOUR TOWELS ON A LOUIS CHAIR UPHOLSTERED IN PUCCI TERRYCLOTH, EVEN IF YOUR BATHROOM IS TINY.

7. NAME YOUR CHILDREN AFTER VENERABLE NEW YORK LAW FIRMS FOR PATRICIAN PANACHE. MY FAVES ARE CADWALLADER, WICKERSHAM, TAFT, DEBVOISE, AND PLIMPTON. HOW CUTE WOULD A LITTLE CADWALLADER ADLER BE?

8. WHEN IN DOUBT, ADD MIRRORS FOR EXTRA GLAMOUR. PUT A PIECE OF MIRROR ON TOP OF A CABINET TO MAKE IT SPARKLE OR IN A NICHE TO CREATE THE ILLUSION OF DEPTH. MIRRORS ARE MAGIC.

...

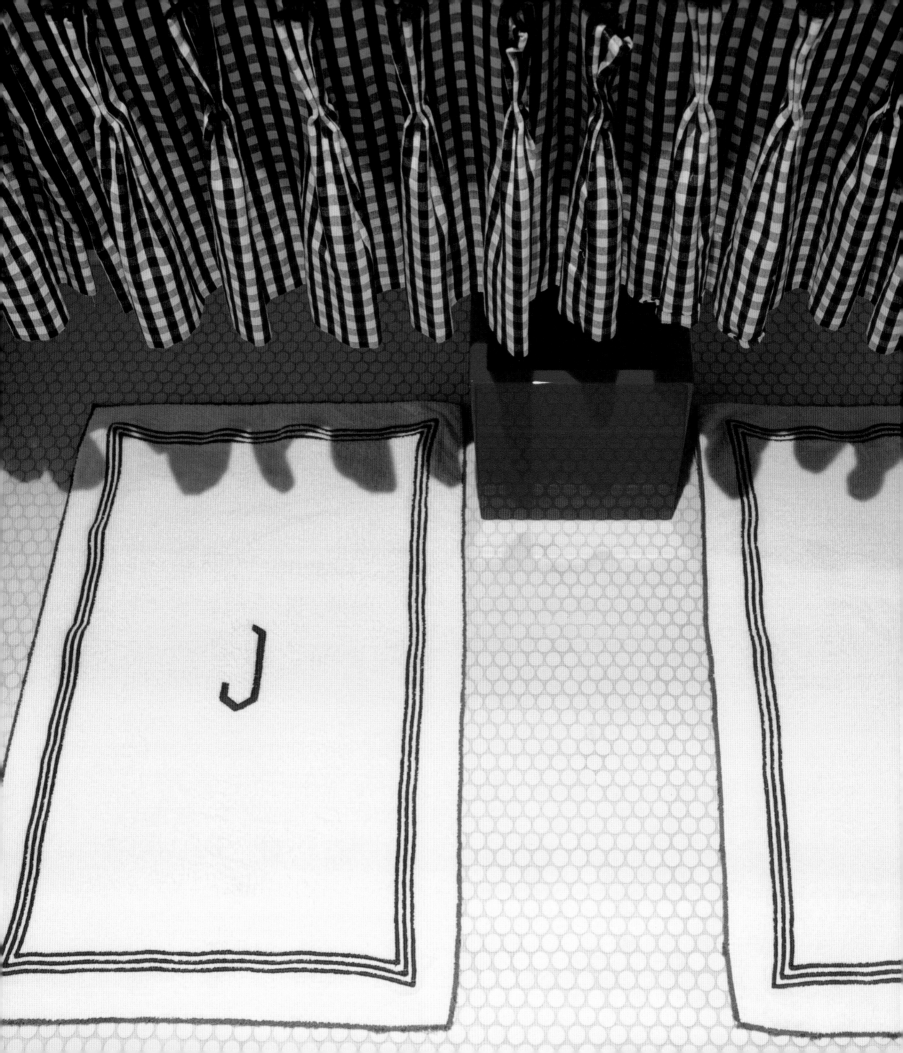

THE STORY
OF MOI:

Mud, Sweat, and Tears

...

THIS APPLE FELL NEAR THE TREE

Not all bourgeois Jewish parents dream that their son will grow up to be a gay potter, but mine rolled with the punches. My parents, Cynthia and Harry, were progressive and creative and all in all pretty great. They even stood by me when, at the age of 24, I quit my job as a junior talent agent and holed up in my fourth-floor walk-up studio for six months to make pots. Even if they may have privately contemplated an intervention, they let me flounder along at my own retarded pace. Imagine their expression when I finally called to say that Barneys had placed an order and I would henceforth be selling pots that took only three days to make for $7 apiece! But I'm getting ahead of myself.

When I was young, we lived in a modern house in a farm town in New Jersey. Our home was a weird fusion of my parents' two very different styles. My father was a rigorous minimalist who created a gallery-like setting where individual objects could shine. My mother is the complete opposite. Her aesthetic is exuberant and chaotic and anything but restrained. She was even game enough to get tarted up and star in a theatrical David LaChapelle photo (opposite). My parents have been total inspirations to me.

Today, I'm happy doing what I do, spreading joy through groovy designs, and it's in no small part thanks to them. But it hasn't always been like this. *Moi* has slaved away to get here, so I thought I'd share my kooky journey. My career has been bumpy, filled with bad advice and wrong turns. (I was nearly fired from almost every job I ever held.) But ultimately, I kept doing what I loved—and prevailed. My hope is that my humble journey will inspire you to listen to your own heart and follow your own dreams.

i become
a man(ish)

Here I am at my bar mitzvah in 1979, surrounded by eight lovely attendees about whom I'm supposed to be dreaming—which, of course, I wasn't. What I'm really thinking about is the potter's wheel that my parents promised me as a bar mitzvah present.

I look back on that day with a top note of melancholy, and it all has to do with the formal Brooks Brothers navy suit I wore. My bar mitzvah occurred just as '70s excess had begun to wane. I saw preppy conservativism on the fashion horizon and, regrettably, I went with it. The year before, I had attended Maury Stein's bar mitzvah, which had an El Al theme. All the Stein men wore purple velvet three-piece suits with open collars. Floral centerpieces mimicked airplanes, and the waitresses were dressed like stewardesses. I have learned that you should always dress in an excessively trendy way, so that you can look back on pictures of yourself and realize that you were fully engaged with the culture of the time. (By the way, Maury's father was a podiatrist, and they had a pool shaped like a foot.)

180

ONE OF THE GREATEST THINGS ABOUT BEING A POTTER THROUGHOUT HIGH SCHOOL WAS THAT I COULD MAKE MY OWN BONGS. NOWADAYS, I'M MORE LIKELY TO USE ONE OF MY TEAPOTS.

i was a teenage potter

I first tried pottery at summer camp when I was twelve. I'd gone to camp to be a vital athlete, but then I laid eyes on the super-foxy pottery teacher and decided to take his class instead. The minute I touched clay, I was obsessed. I spent the entire summer in the pottery studio in a clay-spattered Rush concert tee. My parents came to pick me up at the end of the summer expecting to find a tan, vigorous soccer star, but instead they found a pale potter with a dream.

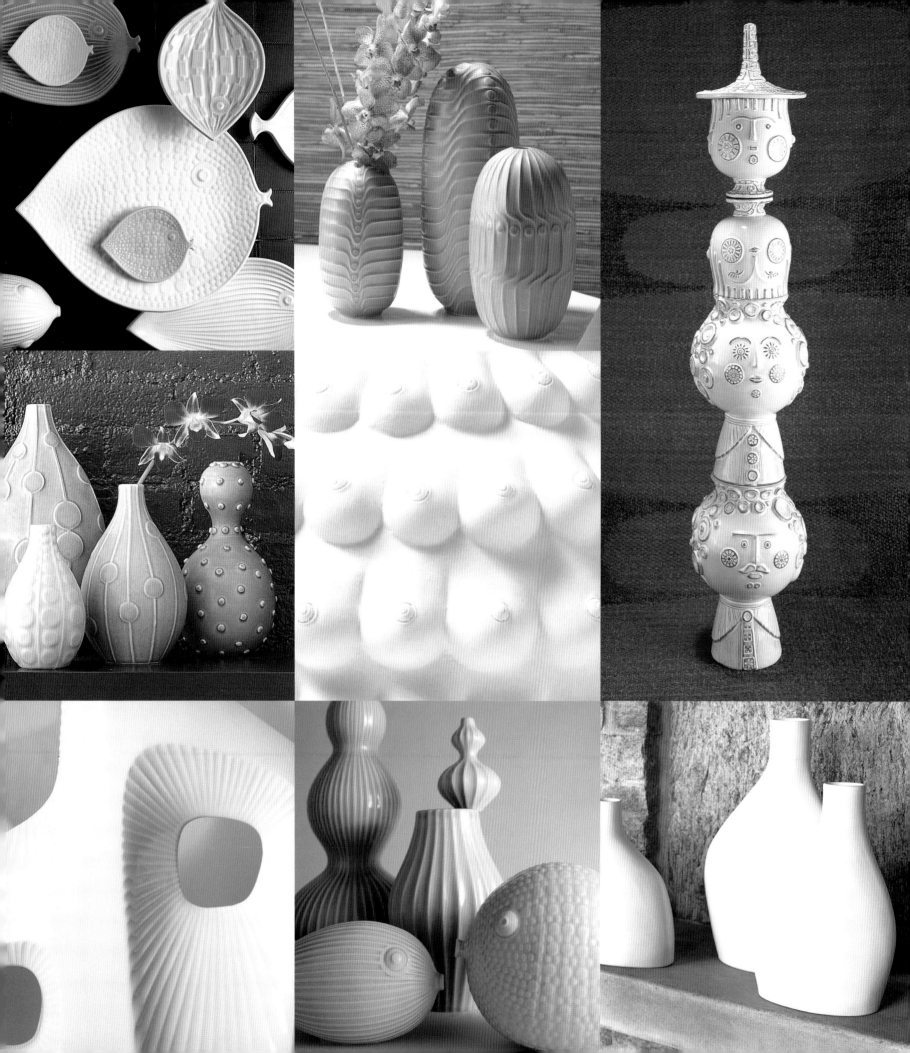

I MADE THESE POTS (MY COUTURE COLLECTION) ON THE WHEEL AND THEN APPLIED RELIEF PATTERNS. THE AORTA VASE (SECOND FROM RIGHT) STARTS AS AN EGG-SHAPED POT, AND THEN I TURN IT ON ITS SIDE AND ATTACH THE SPOUTS. WHEN I MADE THIS GROUP, I WAS THINKING OF THE ORNATE MODERNIST ARCHITECTURE OF EDWARD DURELL STONE AND THE MATTE WHITE FINISH OF HIS BUILDINGS. DURELL STONE (DESIGNER OF THE INFAMOUS LOLLIPOP BUILDING IN NEW YORK'S COLUMBUS CIRCLE) FUSED CLEAN LINES WITH A LAYER OF PATTERN AND DECORATION THAT WAS A SLAP IN THE FACE TO FORM-FOLLOWS-FUNCTION MODERNISTS.

early career advice: you suck

I allegedly studied semiotics and art history at Brown University but really spent my time at the nearby Rhode Island School of Design making pots. It being the '80s, I was obsessed with materialism, early rap music, and fashion. I decided to channel these interests into my ceramic oeuvre. When I look at my old pieces now, I think, "I was quite a little visionary." But my hippie-dippy professor thought otherwise. "You have no talent," she told me. "Move to New York and become a lawyer."

If my three years as an assistant to harpy-ish shrews in the entertainment industry had been any less miserable, I might have clawed my way up to become a mid-level talent agent with a heart of coal. (Or not, as I was a horrible employee who yapped on the phone all day with friends.) Instead I bottomed out, quit my job, and had a revelation: The approval of my evil pottery professor meant nothing. I had to do what I loved, which meant making pots that I myself would want to buy.

i believe good design creates good moods

When most people think of pottery, they think of a lonely potter, sequestered in a garret, making the same mug over and over as the rest of the world passes him by.

When I first started making my pots, I wanted them to be colorful and graphic and fun. As my sensibility evolved to incorporate a more rustic approach and a Palm Beach-y twinkle, I strived to maintain the anti-depressive spirit of my early pots. In my pots and my pillows and everything I do, I am obsessed with fusing serious craftsmanship with happy iconography.

Sometimes it seems that designers have to be a bit dour and abstruse in order to be taken seriously. I love popular artists like Bjorn Wiinblad and Leroy Neiman who make work that is happy and communicative and that speaks to people rather than critics. I want people to see my work and feel good.

187

Marimekko meets Machu Picchu

I spent my pretty years (mid- to late twenties) as a production potter, working feverishly. It was a weird period in my life. I would get up at 6 a.m., go to the studio, make a hundred mugs, and then come home and fall asleep. I repeated this routine seven days a week, for about three years. While trapped behind the wheel, I dreamed of all the things that I hoped to do—if I could only get out from behind that damn wheel! It was during this time that all my nefarious plans were hatched.

In 1995, I hooked up with an organization called Aid to Artisans, which is a nonprofit that connects designers in America with artisans in developing countries for a PC, non–Kathie Lee Gifford sort of business relationship. Aid to Artisans suggested I visit a workshop in Peru that could make my work. (Needless to say, my Jewish parents were terrified. When I told them I was going to war-torn Peru, my father said, "That's great. Where do you want to be buried?") But off I went and discovered a paradisiacal work-shop by the sea. I spent several months there and established a great relationship that continues to this day. And, by freeing myself from production, I was able to have a creative explosion. While in Peru, I fell in love with South American textiles and started having pillows and throws and rugs made. I fused a Scandinavian modern sensibility that is dear to my heart with the ethnic handcrafted style of Peru. I call this look Marimekko meets Machu Picchu.

We believe our designs are award winning even
though they've never actually won any

world

see what's in store

I opened my first store in SoHo in 1998, then moved to bigger digs in 2004. Many design stores are off-putting ("Don't touch this," "No kids or dogs allowed," "You're not cool enough to shop here"), but in mine we always try to be welcoming. "Enter our groovy world," which is written on the wall in the SoHo store, is an invitation to tuck in to my maximalist design aesthetic, in which different looks—Palm Beach, Hippie, and Mod—coexist in an idiosyncratic mix. I now have six stores—SoHo, Madison Avenue, East Hampton, Miami, Los Angeles, and San Francisco—and am poised on the brink of taking over the world with happy chic.

191

MY SOHO OFFICE IS NOT A TYPICAL DESIGN OFFICE. THOUGH WE HAVE CONFERENCE ROOMS AND LOTS OF OPERATIVES ZOOMING ABOUT MAKING THINGS HAPPEN, THE REAL HEART AND SOUL IS THE POTTERY STUDIO. EVER SINCE I STARTED MAKING POTS, I'VE BEEN PLAGUED BY CLAY DUST, THE INEVITABLE AND VERY MESSY BY-PRODUCT OF MAKING POTTERY. MY MOTHER KVETCHED ABOUT FOOTPRINTS ON THE CARPET WHEN I WAS A TEEN POTTER, AND I'VE BEEN KICKED OUT OF STUDIOS FOR BEING TOO MESSY. UNFORTUNATELY, I SEEM UNABLE TO ESCAPE THIS PROBLEM, AND MY FANCY-PANTS OFFICE IS CONSTANTLY RIDDLED WITH THE EVIDENCE OF MY TRADE.

it's not so lonely at the top

I may have started off as an isolated potter, but now I get to create my own twisted corporate culture. Every day at work brings wild and unexpected fun. And all kinds of projects vie for attention: interior design, new pots and textiles, furniture, lighting, and six retail stores. Most importantly, I get to work with the most incredible posse on earth. I'm surrounded by gifted and creative people, many of whom have a catty streak, thank God. We giggle all day and say inappropriate things, but best of all we're all really serious about design and passionate about creating happy homes.

192

marry a window dresser *and* a norwich terrier

During the recent gay marriage debate, many people argued that if the definition of marriage changes and the floodgates open, what's to stop people from marrying their pets? Simon and I thought, "How fantastic! Finally we can marry each other and Liberace, and the state will recognize our alternative lifestyle!"

Although I've been prattling on and on about how home decorating can change your life, I actually believe that the most important key to a happy home is creating your own family, be it friends, pets, kids, or spouses. I feel like I can take creative risks—and yes, decorating risks—because none of it really matters. I know that at the end of the day, the only thing that matters are my happy times with my window dresser and my Norwich Terrier.

195

My Prescription For :
ANTI-DEPRESSIVE LIVING

3. DECORATE YOUR HOME SO THAT IT EXPRESSES WHO YOU ARE AND MAKES YOU **HAPPY** WHEN YOU WALK IN THE DOOR.

1. WHEN HAVING A DINNER PARTY, ALWAYS **SERVE YOURSELF FIRST.** IT WILL MAKE PEOPLE FEEL MORE COMFY.

2. FIND PEOPLE TO **LOVE AND SHARE** YOUR LIFE WITH. SURRENDER TO YOUR RELATIONSHIPS AND MAKE THEM AS HAPPY AND SWEET AS YOU POSSIBLY CAN.

4. BE A CONTRARIAN. EMBRACE **STRONG POINTS OF VIEW.** CHANGE FROM ONE EXTREME TO THE OTHER IN MID-CONVERSATION TO REALLY STIR THINGS UP.

5. DON'T FEEL GUILTY ABOUT WATCHING TOO MUCH TV.

7. FIND WORK THAT YOU LOVE. DON'T STOP UNTIL YOU FIND IT AND **DON'T LET ANYONE HOLD YOU BACK** OR PUT YOU DOWN.

6. BE WIDELY INFLUENCED. THERE ARE SQUILLIONS OF FUNSTERS DOING GREAT THINGS, AND I GET IDEAS FROM EVERY-WHERE—ARCHITECTURE, ART, REALITY TV, FRIENDS. I READ LIBERAL AND CONSER-VATIVE WRITERS. I'M INSPIRED BY STREET FASHION AND NATURE. I THINK YOU SHOULD ALWAYS EXPLORE AND BE OPEN TO NEW EXPERIENCES. **EXPOSE YOURSELF.**

8. OBEY EVERY COMMAND IN THIS BOOK. **OR DON'T.** I WANT YOU TO DO WHAT-EVER MAKES YOU HAPPY.

...

acknowledgments

PHOTO CREDITS: ALL IMAGES COPYRIGHT © ANNIE SCHLECHTER, EXCEPT THE FOLLOWING: PAGES 180-81: COURTESY JONATHAN ADLER; PAGES 8-9, 122, 123, 164-65, AND 172-73: COPYRIGHT © RICHARD BARNES; PAGE 74 AND 75 (TOP): COURTESY THE BONNIE CASHIN COLLECTION, CHARLES E. YOUNG RESEARCH LIBRARY, DEPARTMENT OF SPECIAL COLLECTIONS, UCLA; PAGES 44 AND 45 (BOTTOM): COPYRIGHT © CORBIS; PAGE 35: COPYRIGHT © TODD EBERLE; PAGE 193 (TOP RIGHT): COPYRIGHT © ANDREW FRENCH; PAGE 26 (BOTH): COURTESY ANDREW GOLDSTEIN; PAGES 11, 98-99, 101, AND 102: COPYRIGHT © ART GRAY; PAGES 19, 29 (RIGHT), 104, 105, 108-109, AND 114-15: COPYRIGHT © MICHAEL GRIMM; PAGE 188 (BOTH): COURTESY DEB HAYES; PAGE 170 (BOTH): COPYRIGHT © HULTON ARCHIVE/GETTY IMAGES; PAGES 46-47: COPYRIGHT © DEBORAH KALAS; PAGES 24, 56-57, 58, 130 (TOP LEFT AND BOTTOM MIDDLE), 135 (TOP RIGHT), 137, 154, 171, AND 176-77: COPYRIGHT © DEAN KAUFMAN; PAGE 178: COPYRIGHT © DAVID LACHAPELLE; PAGE 62: PHOTOGRAPH BY MICHAEL LUPINO, COURTESY *METROPOLITAN HOME*; PAGES 28, 29 (LEFT), 63, AND 194-95: COPYRIGHT © NGOC MINH NGO; PAGE 106 (ALL): COPYRIGHT © PAUL ROCHELEAU; PAGE 152: COPYRIGHT © RYLAND PETERS & SMALL, PHOTOGRAPHER CATHERINE GRATWICKE; PAGES 12-13, 60-61, 84-85, 89, AND 118: COPYRIGHT © JASON SCHMIDT; PAGES 45 (TOP), 52-53, 68, 96 (RIGHT), 182, 191 (BOTTOM), 192, 193 (TOP LEFT AND BOTTOM): COPYRIGHT © MATTHEW SEPTIMUS; PAGES 30-31, 40, 41, 48-49, 92-93, 96 (LEFT), 127, 134, 136, 156-57, AND 159 (LEFT): COPYRIGHT © ERIC STAUDENMAIER; PAGES 4, 27, 42, 43, AND 150-51: COPYRIGHT © WILLIAM WALDRON

COLLEAGUES: Throughout this book I've said "I did this" or "I did that." It's all lies, lies, lies. The truth is that "We did this" and "We did that." I am lucky to work with the most creative and talented and smart and amusing posse on earth, and everything in this book is the result of our fantastic collaboration. So, thank you to Nilo Alarcon, Mercedita Andrew, Paul Aquino, Erin Carmack, Marlene Cimicato, Theresa Cooper, Morten Evensen, Victoria Evertsz, Ginny Fitzgerald, Jay Fitzgerald, Luis Gonzalez, Carole Grayes, Andrew Greenman, Jennifer Hopwood, Coco Iverson, Allison Julius, Valerie McDermott, Ana Meza, Kristina Milano, Isaias Mora, Daniel Pafford, Jose Rivera, Alex Saleeby, Cain Semrad, Simon Temprel, Miro Terrell, Jerin Tuek, Joe Weiner, Michael Whitton, David Wilhoit, Tricia Wimmer. A very special thank you to the design operatives who help me concoct all of my stuff and who are beyond talented: Darren Brown (genius), Leslie Degler (brilliant), Alice Lam (*j'adore*), Louis Marra (truly a Godsend), Philip O' Sullivan (unbelievable), and Edwin Vera (the most talented person I know).

POSSE: I'm sure everybody thinks that they have the best friends and family on earth, but I know it. So, thank you to Cynthia Adler, Amy Adler and Lenn Robbins and little Harry, David Adler and Vanessa Drucker, Julia Carr Bayler, Belle Benson, Liberace Adler Doonan, Andrew Goldstein and Mrs. Goldstein, Marita "Nanny" Gonzalez, Deb Hayes, Liz and Jeff Lange, Alex May, Biz Mitchell, Mayer Rus, Deb Schwartz, David Sigal and Brad Hoylman, Andrea Stern and Kenny Di Paulo, and Mark Welsh. And, of course, the biggest thank you to my husband, Simon Doonan, for everything.

COLLABORATORS AND SUPPORTERS: I am happy to say that a lot of the people with whom I've crossed paths professionally have become friends. My decorating clients are all bold and creative and inspirational. Many editors have supported *Moi* from day one, and I worship them for that. So, thank you to David Anger, Kate Betts, Dawn Brown, Dominique Browning, Ellen Carey, Marilyn and Eduardo Deneumostier, Tracy Edwards, Beth Fazio, Robert Forrest, Kim France, Adam Glick, Wendy Goodman, Charo Inurritegui, Lisa Jacobson, Suzi Jones, Judy Kameon, Rob Kennedy, Tony Longoria, David Mann, Deborah Needleman, Nancy Novogrod, Linda O'Keeffe, Todd Oldham, Dorothy Rabinowitz, Marianne Rohrlich, Margaret Russell, Ellin Saltzman, Anita Sarsidi, Robin Sayetta, Bill Sofield, Andrea Stern, Rima Suqi, Jacquie and Joel Tractenberg, Julie Turkel, Newell Turner, Pilar Viladis, Jane and Richard Wagman, and Donna Warner.

I'm also honored to work with the grooviest stores on earth and the best licensees. So, thank you to Croscill, Dioni, Elrene, Franco, Mara-mi, Precidio, Rowe, Stitch, Zrike, and everyone at Barneys, especially Howard Socol, Tracey Edwards, and Tom Kalenderian.

BOOK PEEPS: Writing this book has been more fun than I ever imagined, all because of the triumphant book peeps who've provided countless giggles. So, thank you to Judith Regan (*j'adore!*), Jason Puris, Richard Ljoenes, and Cassie Jones at Regan Books; and Charlie Melcher, Duncan Bock (my old chum), Megan Worman (tireless and heavenly), Bonnie Eldon, and Lauren Nathan at Melcher Media. Thanks also to Yael Eisele, Deb Hayes (worship), Rymn Massand, and Annie Schlechter (divine).

Finally, I want to thank my late father, Harry Adler, who was a true inspiration. I wish he could see everything that I'm doing.

Melcher Media wishes to thank David E. Brown, Max Dickstein, Neal Gorevic, Emily Oberman, Alessandra Rafferty, Lia Ronnen, Holly Rothman, Nathan Sayers, Matthew Septimus, Bonnie Siegler, Lindsey Stanberry, Eric Staudenmaier, and Shoshana Thaler.

• • •